ARCHITECTS
and
CIVIL ENGINEERS
of
NINETEENTH CENTURY
SCARBOROUGH

A BIOGRAPHICAL DICTIONARY

by

ANNE & PAUL BAYLISS

ARCHITECTS
and
CIVIL ENGINEERS
of
NINETEENTH CENTURY
SCARBOROUGH

© 2001 A.M. & P.F.C. BAYLISS

ISBN 0 9506405 4 9

Published by
A. M. Bayliss
Flat 5,
12, Esplanade,
Scarborough. YO11 2AF

CONTENTS

ILLUSTRATIONS

All illustrations in this book are reproduced by kind permission of North Yorkshire County Libraries and are from the Print Collection in Scarborough Reference Library.

ALSO BY THE AUTHORS

Photographers in Mid Nineteenth Century Scarborough
by
Anne & Paul Bayliss
ISBN 0 9506405 3 0

Scarborough Artists of the Nineteenth Century
by
Anne & Paul Bayliss
ISBN 0 9506405 2 2

William James Boddy, York Artist (1832-1911)
His Life and Works
by
Anne & Paul Bayliss
ISBN 0 9506405 1 4

The Life and Works of James Trubshaw (1777-1853)
Staffordshire Builder, Architect and Civil Engineer
by
Anne Bayliss
ISBN 0 9506405 0 6

Sir Charles Wolseley (1769-1846)
The Radical Baronet
by
Anne Bayliss
ISBN 0 903363 20 8

FOREWORD

In 1863, the young George Frederick Bodley was high on scaffolding painting the chancel arch of St Martin's church on South Cliff with an involved Tractarian symbolism of pomegranates and sacred monograms. The gas jet lighting his work flared and set fire to his whiskers, causing him to flap about and nearly step backwards into eternity. If he had, Scarborough would have ended prematurely the career of a man who became one of the greatest and most innovative of Victorian architects, and the shape of numerous towns in Britain and abroad would have been very different. This fact tells us how central the remote resort of Scarborough was in its Victorian heyday. Not merely did it attract the best of Victorian architects, it even began one or two great careers, notably that of Thomas Edwin Cooper. Some Scarborough architects, notably the great Frank Tugwell only practised locally, and so his glorious talent was expended to the benefit of Scarborians alone; they constitute a secret local treasure that should be more widely shared. Now the Bayliss's have made this appreciation more possible, and we should thank them for it.

More than most towns, Scarborough has preserved its rich Victorian architectural heritage. Although a number of treasures have been lost in recent years (most notably All Saints, Falsgrave, the Pavilion Hotel and the Bar Church) Scarborough's nineteenth-century building stock remains surprisingly intact, more so than Victorian resorts like Brighton. The relative decline in the town's fortunes in the past century has meant that major urban redevelopment has not occurred. The tendency now is to preserve and to re-use Victorian buildings, so the Queen Street Convent, the Falsgrave Unitarian Church and (hopefully) Holy Trinity, Westbourne Grove, will survive to greet a new sort of Scarborough visitor: the cultural tourist. Scarborough's nineteenth-century architectural grandeur has now sailed into the twenty-first century, and in this coming century we will see a growing appreciation of the art and imagination of the Victorian architect. So it is that Anne and Paul Bayliss's new work will be a very important guide for lovers (present and future) of Scarborough's architectural heritage.

David Crouch
Professor of History,
University of Hull.

PREFACE

My interest in Scarborough's architecture began at nine years of age, when my teacher, Mr Raymond Fieldhouse, drew his class's attention to the massive, blank, brick wall at the rear of the recently enlarged Woolworth's store on Vernon Road. I will always be grateful to him because he had taught me to look around and take an interest in my surroundings and to understand that a quality environment does not just happen. Thankfully the wall has now been incorporated into the Brunswick Pavilion.

Concern for the built environment is at the core of the activities of a Civic Society, so I think that it is entirely appropriate that we should support this excellent work. I was concerned, as a civil engineer, to be writing a preface for a book about architects, but reassured to find that engineers of the calibre of Sir John Coode are also included. For me, Victorian confidence and vigour leaps out of the dictionary entries.

Reading this book made me want to get out and about and look at Scarborough's buildings, using all the carefully researched information to help my appreciation. I was intrigued to learn that the man responsible for the Grand Hotel spent his later years working as a penniless waiter in Paris. Also that in 1821 John McAdam was appointed to 'put the York to Scarborough road into a competent state of affairs to hold out inducements to travellers more frequently to visit Scarborough'.

In the 'Streets of Scarborough', published by the Civic Society in 1973, Raymond Fieldhouse and John Barrett wrote:

'While not closing our minds to the validity of some change, nor advocating adherence to a rigid policy of preservation, we should seek to conserve what is good and bear in mind that the price of amenity is eternal vigilance.'

I am sure that this book will help us to appreciate what is good and thereby make Scarborough a better place to live, to work in and visit.

Scarborough and District Civic Society are very pleased to support this new work by Anne and Paul Bayliss.

Peter Cooper , Chairman,

Scarborough & District Civic Society
(founded 1964)
P.O.Box 151 , Scarborough YO12 4YJ

INTRODUCTION

This is a book about people, the men (alas there were no women) who designed the major public buildings of nineteenth century Scarborough. Several pictorial books have been published about the buildings themselves, but they make little or no reference to the architects. Occasionally a name is stated, but this raises more questions than it answers. Who was this man? Did he have a practice in Scarborough or did he come from elsewhere? Why was he chosen for this particular building? Did he win a competition for the design or was he chosen because of some particular skill or expertise? Did he design any other buildings in Scarborough or elsewhere? What is known about his background? Where did he train or study?

We hope that this book helps to answer these and similar questions. Although entitled a "dictionary" it is also a directory in the sense that it aims to direct the reader to sources of further information. To this end a comprehensive list of references has been included.

The original concept of the book was limited to the architects of nineteenth century Scarborough but this definition soon became blurred.

Firstly, the term "architect" was too limiting. In the first half of the nineteenth century the distinction between architects, surveyors, builders and indeed other trades such as masons was not clear-cut. To exclude some of these would have missed out several important buildings. Further, it soon became clear that some Scarborough "buildings" such as bridges, piers, harbours and towers were designed not by architects but by civil engineers. These needed to be included.

Secondly, the limitation of "nineteenth century" needed definition. Was the building to be erected in the 1800s, or the designer to be born and active in that century? We took a pragmatic approach to this question and thus the time scale is somewhat of our own choosing, at least towards the end of the century. Further did the man have to have designed a building in Scarborough to be included? Generally we said 'yes' except where this would exclude an important man born or trained in Scarborough but who did no work here. Such was Henry Hare, a Scarborian, who became President of the Royal Institute of British Architects, the acme of the profession, who could hardly be left out. As in our biographical dictionary of Scarborough artists it would have been unthinkable to exclude Lord Leighton merely because he never worked in the town although he was born here.

Thirdly, how strictly should we adopt the limitation of "public building"? Again a practical approach was taken. Information about private residences is less available to the researcher than public ones, but rigidly to exclude the domestic would in some instances do an injustice to some of these men.

We have, of course, striven for accuracy, but given that there are about 140 entries in the dictionary there may well be errors. We apologise to our readers for any such defaults that they find and we hope they will bring them to our attention so they may be rectified, at least in our database.

Anne M. Bayliss B.Sc.
Paul F. C. Bayliss LLB. MRCP (Lond.)
(July 2001)

Rotunda Museum (1829) by R.H.Sharpe (see pg 73)
Spa bridge (1827), J.Outhett engineer (see pg 57)

ACKNOWLEDGEMENTS

We would like to thank Mr Bryan Berryman and his staff at Scarborough Reference Library for access to source material in the "Scarborough Room", Jackie Thompson and her staff at Scalby Library for arranging many (and usually obscure) inter-library loans, and Mr Chris Hall, Conservation Officer, Scarborough Borough Council for access to early Urban Sanitary Authority ledgers.

We would also like to thank the many libraries in the British Isles, Ireland and the USA whose staff have provided information including the following; Luke Atkins, Bournemouth Reference Library; Tricia Barnfield, Rawtenstall Library; Siân Collins, Shropshire Records and Research Centre; Sarah Donaldson, Hull Local History Library; Joanna Filligan, National Library of Ireland, Dublin; Kirsty Forbes, National Archives of Scotland; Alan Franklin, Manx National Heritage, Isle of Man; Eleanor Gawne, RIBA Library; Pat Haywood, Institute of Advanced Architectural Studies Library, Kings Manor, York; Rita Hughes, Rhyl Library; Marilyn Ibach, Library of Congress, Washington DC; Pat McNicol, Edinburgh City Archives; Eleanor Nannestad, Lincoln Central Library; Jane Oldfield, RIBA Library; Elizabeth Pettitt, Flintshire Record Office; Peter Ransome, Great Yarmouth Library; T.D.W.Reid, Stockport Central Library: Patricia Sheldon, Newcastle City Library; Stef Stephenson, Patents Information Unit, Leeds; Lynn Wilman, Central Library Lancaster; and staff at the Armitt Library, Ambleside, the Carnegie Library, Harrogate and the Irish Architectural Archives in Dublin.

Particular thanks go to Carol Morgan, archivist at the Institution of Civil Engineers.

We also acknowledge information provided by Charles Braithwaite, Mr & Mrs D.Bryden, Mrs Chaplin, Mr G. Colley, Mick Jefferson, Rose Povey, Mrs Lynne Reed, Peter Robson of Green Lane, Peter Robson of Redscar Lane, Mrs D. Stern and Frank White, all of Scarborough, Caroline Gerard of Edinburgh and Philip Mason of Sharow.

Thanks also go to Emma Bayliss (and Kira) for proof reading the text.

Anne & Paul Bayliss (July 2001)

NOTES ON THE USE OF THIS DICTIONARY

NAMES
The main body of the text is arranged in alphabetical order by surname.
An index of other names and places is to be found at the end of the book.

BUILDINGS
An index to buildings in the form of a table immediately follows these notes.

DATES
The years given immediately after a name are the dates (and places) of birth and death where known.

fl. in connection with an architectural partnership indicates the years during which the firm was active.

fl.Sc. indicates the years an architect/engineer was active in Scarborough.

post indicates the latest date that an individual has been identified as living.

SCARBOROUGH WORK
This is list of the main buildings in Scarborough for which the architect/ engineer was responsible. The associated dates indicate the year of completion or opening of the building.

ADDRESSES
All addresses are in Scarborough unless otherwise stated.

REFERENCES
(number) indicates the number of the reference(s) used in compiling the biographical note. A full list of these references is given at the end of the book. Extensive use of newspapers, periodicals, directories, and census records was made while researching this book. Space precludes listing each date for such references, although their titles are included.

SCARBOROUGH BUILDINGS LIST

1. (*)   indicates building no longer standing
2. (**) indicates building now has a new use
3. name of building is that at time of completion
4. dates refer to completion or opening of building
N.B. *This is not a complete listing of all the buildings mentioned in the text but includes the more representative ones.*

CHURCHES & CHAPELS

Church of England

*All Saints, Falsgrave Rd	built	1868	George Bodley
*Christ Church, Vernon Place	built	1828	Peter Atkinson
	restn.	1873	Charles Bury
Holy Trinity, Westbourne Grove	built	1880	Ewan Christian
St James Chapel Seamer Lane	built	1883	Paley & Austin
	enlgd.	1894	Paley & Austin
**St Johns Mission, St Sepulchre St	built	1884	Charles H Fowler
St Martins, South Cliff	built	1863	George Bodley
	enlgd	1879	George Bodley
St Mary's Parish Church	restn	1852	Ewan Christian
St Michaels, Wheatcroft	built	1880	George Bodley
*St Paul's Mission, Regent St	built	1879	Charles Bury
*St Saviours (temp), Gladstone Rd	built	1898	John C. Hawes
St Saviours Church, Gladstone Rd	built	1902	J.T.Micklethwaite
**St Thomas, East Sandgate	built	1840	Thomas Davison
	enlgd	1859	John Petch
	restn	1889	Charles H Fowler

Methodist

*Chapel, St Sepulchre St	built	1865	Joseph Wright
*Jubilee Chapel, Aberdeen Walk	built	1861	William B.Stewart
**Prim. Meth. Chapel, Seamer Rd	built	1904	J.Caleb Petch
*Prim. Meth. Chapel, St John's Rd	built	1869	J & D Petch
*St John's Rd Chapel	built	1880	Godfrey Peacock
South Cliff Chapel, Ramshill Rd	built	1886	William J. Morley
**United Free Chapel, Castle Rd	built	1860	Thomas Simpson
*Wesleyan Chapel, Queen St	built	1840	James Simpson
Wesleyan Chapel, Seamer Rd	built	1878	David Petch
Westborough Chapel	built	1862	William B. Stewart
Wesleyan Church, Hoxton Rd	built	1905	F.A.Tugwell

Roman Catholic

St Edward's, Avenue Victoria	built	1913	John Petch & Son
St Peter's, Castle Rd	built	1858	George Goldie

Congregational

*Bar Church	built	1850	Raffles Brown
	enlgd	1873	John Petch
**Eastborough	built	1869	Paull & Robinson
*Manor Rd	built	1898	J.Caleb Petch
Ramshill Rd	built	1865	Lockwood & Mawson

Others

Baptist Church, Albemarle Cres.	built	1867	Lockwood & Mawson
Baptist Church, Columbus Ravine	built	1911	J.Caleb Petch
Dean Rd Cemetery Chapels	built	1856	Pritchett & Sons
*Friends Meeting Ho., York Place	built	1894	Stark & Rowntree
Salvation Army, Alma Parade	built	1881	John Hall
**Seamans Institute, Sandside		1897	J.Caleb Petch
*Temperance Hall, North St	built	1868	J & D Petch
**Temperance Hall, Scalby	built	1894	Stark & Rowntree
**Unitarian Church, Falsgrave Rd	built	1876	Charles A.Bury

SCHOOLS

**Adult Schl., St Sepulchre St	built	1894	Stark & Rowntree
**Adult Schl., Roscoe St	built	1903	Fred Rowntree
**Amicalbe Society's Schools	built	1865	William B.Stewart
*Art Schl, Vernon Place	convn.	1884	John Hall
**Board Schl, Falsgrave	built	1872	William Watson
Board Schl. Friarage	built	1896	J.Caleb Petch
*Board Schl. Trafalgar St W.	built	1873	Stewart & Bury
**Board Schl. Long Westgate	convn.	1873	Stewart & Bury
Gladstone Road Schl.	built	1890	Hall & Tugwell
*National Schl. Girls, Queen St	built	1836	John Thompson
*National Schl. Boys, Queen St	built	1837	John Thompson
**St Martin's Gram. Ramshill Rd	built	1872	George Bodley
*St Martins Ch. Schl Royal Ave	built	1898	Messrs Tugwell
**School, Filey Rd	built	1909	Fred Rowntree
Scarborough College, Filey Rd	built	1898	Hall, Cooper & Davis
Higher Grade Schl., Westwood	built	1900	Hall, Cooper & Davis
*Sunday Schl. Bar Church	built	1862	John Petch
*Sunday Schl., Queen St Chapel	built	1879	William Watson

CIVIC BUILDINGS

*TownHall, Castle Rd	convn.	1870	Thomas Raper
*Courts & Police Stn. Castle Rd	convn.	1870	Thomas Raper
Town Hall (from1903)	built	1852	Henry Wyatt
Market Hall, St Helens Sq.	built	1853	John Irvin
**GPO, Huntriss Row	built	1881	James Williams
Rotunda Museum	built	1829	Richard H.Sharp
Rotunda Museum	enlgd.	1885	John Petch
Scarborough Spa:-			
Sea wall & promenade		1830s	James Leslie
Cliff stabilisation		1840s	James Leslie
*Gothic saloon	built	1839	Henry Wyatt
*Gothic saloon	extn.	1845	Henry Wyatt
Gardens & drainage		1840	George Knowles
*Grand Hall & gardens	built	1857	Joseph Paxton
*Observation Tower	built	1860	Jospeh Paxton
New Spa buildings	built	1880	Verity & Hunt
Bandstand & café	built	1913	T.E.Cooper

HOSPITALS & BATHS

**Cottage Hosp., Spring Hill Rd	built	1870	William Barry
**Cottage Hosp., Spring Hill Rd	extn.	1897	William E.Barry
*Dispensary, Elder St	built	1858	William Barry
**Hydropathic Estab. Spring Bank	built	1889	J.Caleb Petch
*Hospital & Disp., Friars Entry	built	1893	Hall & Tugwell
**Northern Sea Bathing Infirmary	built	1860	William B.Stewart
**Phthisis Hosp. at Workhouse	built	1911	James A.Iveson
**Public Baths, Blands Cliff	built	1859	Josiah F.Fairbank
*Vernon Place Baths	built	1883	Charles A.Bury

INSTITUTIONS

**Workhouse, Dean Rd	built	1859	G.& H.Styan
**Workhouse, Dean Rd	addns	1897	Barry & Tugwell
**Workshouse, Dean Rd	offices	1900	Runton & Barry
**Workshouse, Dean Rd	hosp.	1911	James A.Iveson
**Gaol, Dean Rd.	built	1866	William B.Stewart
*Newborough Bar	built	1847	John Barry
Dr Horne's Homes, Londesbro' Rd	built	1908	Henry A.Chapman
Trinity House, St Sepulchre St	built	1832	Richard H.Sharp
*Wheelhouse & Buckle Dwellings	built	1865	William B.Stewart

Wilson's Homes, Castle Rd	built	1836	John Barry
*Model Lodgings, William St	built	1897	J.Caleb Petch
**Convent, Queen St	built	1884	F.A.Walters
Constitutional Club, Huntriss Row	built	1888	Henry A.Cheers
**Liberal Club, Westborough	built	1894	Hall & Tugwell
Masonic Lodge, St Nicholas Cliff	convn.	1884	David Petch
**YMCA, Westborough	mods	1896	J.Caleb Petch

ENTERTAINMENT, CULTURE, SPORT ETC.

*North Cliff Rock Gardens	built	1860	Josiah F.Fairbank
*Aquarium & People's Palace	built	1875	Eugenius Birch
Baths, offices etc.	added	1884	John Petch
Swimming baths	added	1893	Charles Edeson
Theatre	added	1895	Charles Edeson
*Exhibition Hall, Foreshore	built	1895	J.Caleb Petch
Picture Hall, North Marine Rd	built	1912	James Petch
*Entertainment Hall, N.Marine Rd	built	1910	Frank Baker
*Circus, St Thomas St	built	1876	John Petch
*Theatre Royal, St Thomas St	refurb.	1860	George Middlemiss
*Skating Rink, Scalby Rd	built	1909	Thomas C.Barker
Café, Castle by the Sea	added	1913	Thomas C.Barker
Scarborough Cricket Club			
Refreshment room	added	1878	John Petch
Pavilion	built	1894	Hall & Tugwell
Pavilion	built	1903	Charles Edeson
South Cliff Tennis Club			
Ground & pavilion	built	1885	John Petch

COMMERCIAL, INDUSTRIAL ETC.

Banks

Woodall & Co St Nicholas St	built	1864	Henry Wyatt
London Yorkshire, Westboro.	built	1890	Hall & Tugwell
*Albert Hall, Aberdeen Walk	built	1878	John Hall
**Carriage works, Swan Hill Rd	built	1889	Walter Hanstock
*Coastguard House, Foreshore	built	1890	Hall & Tugwell
"Co-op" premises, Victoria Rd	rebld	1897	J.Caleb Petch
Fish Salesmens' offices, West pier	built	1886	Hall & Tugwell
Marshall Ho., St Nicholas St	built	1869	J.& D.Petch
Rowntree's Warehouse, Wooler St	built	1884	Edeson & Rowntree
**J.Rowntree Café, 11, Westboro	convn.	1896	Stark & Rowntree
**Sandside Coffee House,	built	1882	Fred Rowntree

*W Rowntree Store, Westboro	built	1882	Edward Burgess
*Sarony's Studio, South Cliff	built	1858	J.& D.Petch
Scarb. Merc. Off.s, Aberdeen Walk	built	1882	John Hall

HOTELS

Alexandra (Clifton), North Cliff	built	1864	J.& D.Petch
Belmont Terr. (Esplanade Hotel)	built	1845	John Gibson
Crown Hotel, Esplanade	built	1845	John Gibson
Grand Hotel, St Nicholas Cliff	built	1867	Cuthbert Brodrick
Grand Hotel Refreshment Rooms	added	1871	William B.Stewart
*Pavilion Hotel	built	1870	Stewart & Bury
Royal Hotel, Harcourt Place	extn.	1862	Henry Wyatt

PRIVATE HOUSES & VICARAGES

"Belvedere", Esplanade	built	1885	Frederick W. Roper
"Brackencliffe", Esplanade Cres.	built	1905	Walter Brierley
"Brookholme", Holbeck Hill	built	1899	Frank A.Tugwell
** "Dunollie", Filey Rd	built	1901	Penty & Penty
"Endcliffe", Granville Rd	built	1888	Edeson & Rowntree
"Fairholme", 9, Valley Rd	built	1891	Charles Edeson
* "Hertford House", Filey Rd	built	1903	Runton & Barry
* "Holbeck Hirst", Esplanade	built	1889	Hall & Tugwell
"Langford & Weston", Westwood	built	1863	David Petch
"Lynwood Lodge", 16 Filey Rd	built	1883	Charles A.Bury
** "May Lodge", Filey Rd	built	1885	Edward J.May
"Netherbank", Filey Rd	built	1883	James Demaine
** "St Nicholas Ho." (Town Hall)	built	1852	Henry Wyatt
"Normanton Rise", Holbeck Hill	built	1894	Hall & Tugwell
"Red Court", Esplanade	built	1900	Bedford & Kitson
"Riseborough", Weaponess Park	built	1898	Fred Rowntree
"Seacroft Mansions", Filey Rd	built	1901	Hall, Cooper & Davis
"Shortlands", Filey Rd	built	1883	James Demaine
"Stamford House", Westwood	built	1864	J.& D.Patch
"The Towers", 170, Castle Rd	built	1866	William B.Stewart
Villa, 50, Westbourne Park	built	1886	Edeson & Rowntree
*"Wheatcroft Cliff"(Holbeck Hall)	built	1878	John D.Sedding
"Wheatcroft Towers", Filey Rd	built	1908	John Petch & Son

Vicarages

All Saints, Falsgrave Rd	built	1891	Paley & Austin
**Holy Trinity, 10, Oriel Cres.	built	1896	J.Caleb Petch
St Martins, South Cliff	built	1868	George Bodley

CIVIL ENGINEERING

Bridges

Spa Bridge	opened 1827	John Outhett
Spa Bridge	enlgd. 1880	Thomas Shields
Valley Bridge	opened 1865	Edwin Clark

Harbour

Improvements	engineer		William Chapman
*Brick lighthouse	built	1806	Robert Nixon
West Pier	built	1822	William Barry
Improvements	engineer	1820s	Thomas Blackett
West Pier extensions	built	1881	John Howkins
West Pier extensions	built	1881	Robert S.Wyld
Fish Salesmen's offices	built	1886	Hall & Tugwell
*North Bay Promenade Pier	built	1869	Eugenius Birch
*Warwick's Revolving Tower	built	1898	Hall, Cooper & Davis
*Warwick's Revolving Tower	built	1898	Thomas Warwick

Railways & Tramways

Scarborough Railway Station	built	1845	George T.Andrews
*Forge Valley Railway	engineer		Eugenius Birch
*Scarborough-Whitby Railway	engineer		Eugenius Birch
South Cliff Tramway	built	1875	Richard Hunt
South Cliff Tramway	built	1875	William H.Lucas
South Cliff Tramway	built	1875	Stewart & Bury
*Queen's Parade Tramway	built	1878	Henry P.Holt
Central Cliff Tramway	built	1881	Charles A.Bury
Central Cliff Tramway	built	1881	Thomas F.Morgan

THE DICTIONARY

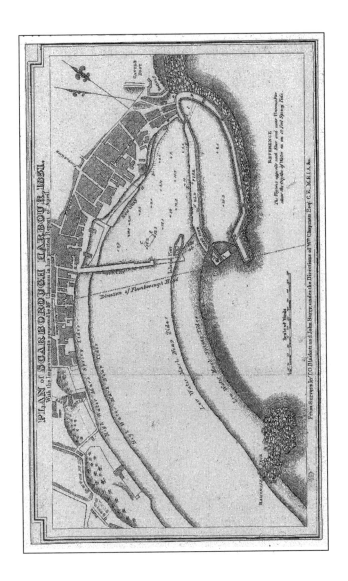

Plan of Scarborough Harbour (1831) by T.O.Blackett (pg 13), J Barry (pg 6) & W. Chapman (pg 19)

2

ABERNETHY, James   **Scottish civil engineers**
James Abernethy (1814 Aberdeen - 1896 Broadstairs)
James Abernethy (1844 Aberdeen - 1897 Margate)
fl.Sc 1895

Scarborough work - (associated with) Marine Drive (1895).

Scarborough's Marine Drive was opened in 1908 after a construction period of 11 years. An article in the Scarborough Mercury in 1908 listed the engineers associated with the project and included James Abernethy who was involved in 1895. There were two James Abernethys, father and son, who worked in partnership on harbour works throughout the world.
References – (14), (64), (85k), (92c).

ANDREWS, George Townsend   **York architect**
1805 (Exeter) - 1855

Scarborough work - Scarborough Railway station (1845), architect to the Scarborough Public Market Company (1853).

George Townsend Andrews studied at the Royal Academy Schools in London in 1825 where, in 1847 and 1848 he exhibited some of his architectural drawings. In 1827 he became established in Castle Gate, York, firstly as an assistant to the London architect Peter Frederick Robinson (1776-1858) and then independently from about 1834. G.T. Andrews became a Fellow of the Institute of British Architects in 1836 having being proposed by Robinson.

George Townsend Andrews was a friend of the York railway speculator George Hudson (1800-71) who promoted the idea that the York and North Midland Railway Company should build a line from York to Scarborough. Andrews became architect to the line being responsible for most of the buildings including Scarborough Railway Station (1845). One further role in Scarborough for G.T.Andrews came in 1853 when he was appointed architect to Scarborough Public Market Company on the death of John Irvin (q.v.) who had designed the new Market Hall but had died before its opening.

As well as his many railway buildings, which included Stations at Whitby (1847) and York (1840-42), G.T.Andrews also designed several churches in Yorkshire including St Stephen's, Acomb (1834); All Saints, Newton-on-Ouse (1849); Holy Evangelists, Shipton-by-Beningborough (1849); St Lawrence's, Flaxton-on-the-Moor (1853-54); St Cuthbert's, Overton (1855) and St Columba's, Topcliffe (1855). Secular buildings by Andrews in York include, St Leonard's Place Crescent including the De Grey Rooms

(Robinson & Andrews 1844-45) and St John's College (original building 1841-46).

George Townsend Andrews died in 1855.

References—(20), (21), (23), (26), (36b), (42), (44), (48), (54), (70), (85j), (92a), (92c), (95), (101), (102).

ATKINSON, Peter (junior)   **York architect**
1776 - 1842 (Calcutta)

Scarborough work - Christ Church, Vernon Place (built 1826-28, demolished 1979).

Peter Atkinson was the son, pupil and later partner of York architect Peter Atkinson (1725-1805). From 1805 to 1819 he was in partnership with Matthew Phillips (c.1781-1825), after which Phillips went into practice on his own. Peter Atkinson then took his own former pupil Richard Hey Sharp (q.v.) into a partnership that lasted until 1827. Later Atkinson was assisted by his sons John (1797-1874) and William (1811-86).

During the period 1821 to 1831 Peter Atkinson designed several new churches in the West Riding of Yorkshire. He was also for many years surveyor to the Corporation of York and was responsible for many buildings in the City including the gaol, the Ouse Bridge, the Foss Bridge and the Layerthorpe Bridge. In York City Art Gallery there is a portrait by Martin Archer Shee (1769-1850) showing Peter Atkinson holding plans of the Ouse Bridge.

In Scarborough, Peter Atkinson designed Christ Church, Vernon Place, which was built between 1826 and 1828, and later enlarged in 1873 by Charles A.Bury (q.v.).

Atkinson retired in 1836 and died in Calcutta on the 13th January 1843.

References – (21), (26), (36b), (46), (85m), (92a), (92b), (92c), (101), (104), (109).

AUSTIN, James   **civil engineer**
1796 (Devon) - post 1868
fl.Sc 1867-68

Scarborough work - none known.

James Austin, builder, surveyor and civil engineer, and Daniel Climie, civil engineer and contractor (q.v.) are separately listed in the 1867 directory for Scarborough at 120, North Marine Road. In the 1851 census for Shrewsbury James Austin is listed as a visitor at Daniel Climie's residence. In 1868 an architectural competition was held for a design for an extension

to the west side of Scarborough Harbour. J.Austin was one of 23 who submitted plans with estimates as was D.Climie, both using a Scarborough address, but the competition was won by Mr C.W.Whittaker of London.
References – (14), (36a), (57), (85j).

AYTOUN, Robert   **civil engineer**
1846 (Hastings) - post 1891
fl. Sc 1887-91

Scarborough work - Royal Albert Drive (1887-90).

Robert Aytoun trained as a civil engineer under Philip Messent (q.v.) and later specialised in harbour work initially in Scotland. Between 1883 and 1885 he worked in Brazil.
In 1887 Aytoun was appointed by Scarborough Corporation to replace Whately Eliot (q.v.) as resident engineer to the project to improve the north cliff and construct Royal Albert Drive. While working in Scarborough Aytoun was consulted on the state of the harbour and gave an estimate of £6,000 for the work needed. However, the local authority wanted a second opinion and consulted his old teacher P.J.Messent whose report was generally adopted.
Robert Aytoun, who was an Associate Member of the Institution of Civil Engineers, described some of his engineering work in Scarborough in a paper entitled "Securing the North Cliff, Scarborough" in the Institution's Minutes of the Proceedings (1890/91).
References – (14), (36a), (61), (64), (85j), (93), (114).

BAKER, Frank   **Scarborough architect**
fl.Sc. 20th century

Scarborough work – Entertainment Hall, North Marine Rd (1910).
see also "Davis & Baker".

Frank Baker studied at Scarborough School of Art winning a prize in the building construction section in 1899. He became an architect and entered partnership with Herbert Davis (q.v.) about 1904. The firm of "Davis & Baker" (q.v.) continued until about 1914 their work being mainly domestic, although in 1910 Frank Baker drew up plans for Mr V.L.Reid for an "Entertainment Hall" on North Marine Road. By 1921 Frank Baker MSA was in sole practice at 7. York Place, Scarborough continuing until at least 1939. Frank Baker also had an office at Clegg Street, Oldham.
References – (14), (36a), (85j), (94), (101), (122), (123), (124).

BARKER, Thomas Christopher   **Scarborough architect**
1880 (Whitby) - 1917 (France)

Scarborough work - skating rink, Scalby Rd (1909), cafe at the "Castle by the Sea" (1913).

Thomas Christopher Barker was the son of a mariner who moved his family from Whitby to Scarborough about 1892. Barker studied at Scarborough School of Art where he was amongst the prize winning students between 1894 and 1897. He was articled to the architect J.Caleb Petch (q.v.) and after gaining experience in Nottingham and Long Eaton and passing his qualifying examinations he returned to Scarborough about 1904 where he set up his own architectural practice.

Thomas Barker's work was mainly domestic although he designed a skating rink on Scalby Road for the West End Skating Company (1909) and a cafe at the 'Castle by the Sea' for C.E.Wilkinson (1913). In November 1912 Barker was elected a Conservative councillor for Scarborough North Ward.

Thomas Christopher Barker joined the 7th Batallion of the Yorkshire Regiment in March 1915 and was killed in France on 4th August 1917. He is buried at the War Cemetery in Fampoux, Pas de Calais and his name is on Scarborough's War Memorial on Oliver's Mount.

References – (14), (36a), (85j), (85k), (94), (101), (117), (122).

BARRY, John (senior)   **Scarborough builder/architect**
1803 (Scarborough) - 1866 (Scarborough)

Scarborough work - Monuments in St Mary's Parish Church, Wilson's Mariners' Homes (*1836), Newborough Bar (*1847, demolished 1890). Wyatt's Spa Saloon (**1837-9), Spa promenade and carriage drive (**1850's).
*as architect ** as builder

John Barry (senior) was based in Scarborough from about 1828 to his death in 1866 as an architect, stone mason, building contractor, and brick and stoneware manufacturer, being in partnership from about 1858 with his son John (junior) (q.v.).

As an architect Barry designed the Newborough Bar (1848), St Stephen's Church at Snainton near Scarborough (1835) and Wilson's Mariners' Homes in Castle Road, Scarborough (1836).

As a stonemason Barry was responsible for some memorial tablets in St Mary's Parish Church, Scarborough and others in St Martin's Church at nearby Seamer.

As a building contractor Barry began working at Scarborough Spa in 1828 when he won a contract from the Cliff Bridge Company and continued working there on various projects for the next 30 years including building Henry Wyatt's (q.v.) 'Gothic Saloon'. In the 1850s, with his son John, he designed and built the carriage road and extension of the Spa promenade, the stone (from Staintondale) being delivered directly to the site from barges towed by steam boats. At the same time a sea wall at the Spa was built by the contractor John Shaftoe of York and two of Barry's sons, Thomas and John (q.v.) married two of Shaftoe's daughters.

Barry also obtained contracts outside Scarborough. Early in the 1840s Filey was expanding due to investment by a Birmingham man, John W. Unett and Barry was the contractor for the Crescent (and possibly architect for parts). Further afield Barry gained two large contracts in Scotland, possibly based upon experience he gained in 1831 when he was involved in a survey of Scarborough Harbour under the supervision of William Chapman (q.v.). In the 1840s Barry was working in Arbroath where he had the contract to build a new harbour. Here one of his superintendents was John Petch (1819-97 q.v.). Also in Scotland Barry was contractor for the Victoria Dock in Leith begun in 1847 and opened in 1852. Here his superintendent was his son William Barry (1828-98 q.v.).

John Barry's Scarborough brick and stoneware factory was in Barry's Lane off Seamer Road. During the 1860s the works were much expanded and sanitary wares as well as bricks were manufactured needing powerful steam machinery. One day, in February 1864, a 15 ton, 34 feet long boiler was transported from Scarborough Railway Station to the works on a special truck pulled by 22 horses. There were, of course, complaints about the pollution caused by manufacturing 7-10 million bricks a year near to dwelling houses.

John Barry was a local councillor for the North Ward for many years and Mayor of Scarborough in 1860. He died on 26th November 1866 at his home in Falsgrave.

References – (9), (14), (18), (29), (36a), (36c), (43), (48), (51), (78), (80), (83), (85b), (85f), (85j), (85k), (92c), (106), (116), (118).

BARRY, John (junior)   **Scarborough building contractor**
1831 (Scarborough) - 1910 (Scarborough)

Scarborough work - Bank for Woodall, Hebden & Co., St Nicholas St/
Newborough (1864), South Cliff Congregational Church, Ramshill Rd
(1865), Baptist Chapel, Long Westgate (1866), All Saints Church,
Falsgrave (1867, demolished 1975), Baptist Church, Albemarle Crescent,
(1867), Gaol Cottages, Dean Rd (1868), Spa Grand Hall (1880), Convent
of Ladies of Mary, Queen St (1884), Dispensary and Hospital, Friars Entry
(1891), St Martin's School, Royal Avenue (1898).

John Barry was the son of architect and building contractor John Barry
(1803-1866 q.v.) from whom he learnt his trade. In 1847 he accompanied
his father and brother William (1828-98 q.v.) to Scotland to work on the
Victoria Dock at Leith which was opened in 1852. The obituary to John
Barry (junior) states that he had also worked abroad as a young man. He
assisted his father's business as a contractor including various works at
Scarborough Spa and through this he met his wife Mary Hannah, eldest
daughter of John Shaftoe, a York contractor also working at the Spa. From
1858 John Barry and his father formed a partnership as John Barry & Son
but John (junior) set up on his own in 1862 and after his father's death in
1866 he became the principal building contractor in Scarborough.
An early contract in 1864 for John Barry (junior) was for a new bank for
"Messrs Woodall, Hebden & Co." designed by Henry Wyatt (q.v.). In
1865 he was the contractor for the Congregational Church on South Cliff
designed by "Lockwood & Mawson" (q.v.) where 200 workmen were
employed. The following year he was contractor for Albemarle Baptist
Church also designed by "Lockwood & Mawson".
In 1868 Barry obtained a contract to build a new workhouse at Haslingden,
Lancashire designed by "Lockwood & Mawson" who presumably had
recommended his work. The contract was worth over £20,000.
While working in Lancashire, Barry submitted estimates for alterations to
the old Town Hall in St Nicholas' Street, Scarborough and was awarded the
contract because his was the lowest estimate. However, his father's
colleague John Petch (1819-97 q.v.) claimed that from personal knowledge
of repairing the Town Hall in 1846 he didn't believe Barry could do the
alterations for as little as £490.
Other important buildings in Scarborough for which Barry was contractor
included All Saints Church, Falsgrave by G.F.Bodley (q.v.), the Convent of
the Ladies of Mary in Queen Street by F.A.Walters (q.v.) for £15,000, the
Dispensary and Hospital in Friars' Entry by "Hall & Tugwell" (q.v.) and St
Martin's School by the brothers Frank & Sidney Tugwell (q.v.). Besides
being a contractor John Barry also designed and built some private houses

in Scarborough.

Carrying on his father's tradition of working at Scarborough Spa, John Barry was the main contractor for "Verity & Hunt's" (q.v.) new building erected after the fire of 1876 and Barry was among the leaders in the grand procession for the re-opening in 1880.

As late as 1902, aged 71, John Barry was advertising as a "Contractor, General Builder, Surveyor and Licensed Assessor" from his Westbrook Building Works. Barry was active in local politics being a member of the Town Council for many years. He died suddenly at home in Prospect Road, Scarborough on November 17th 1910.

References - (3), (14), (18), (36a), (45), (49), (75), (94), (85a), (85c), (85j), (85k), (118).

BARRY, William   Scarborough harbour engineer
1783 – 1838 (Scarborough).

Scarborough work - Western Pier (*1819-22), Harbour engineer 1824 - 1838.
* with Hovington.

William Barry was a stonemason by trade with premises at High Westgate, Scarborough. Between 1819 and 1822, he and a Mr Hovington built the west pier at Scarborough Harbour. By 1822 William Barry was sub-engineer at Scarborough Harbour and in 1824 he replaced the previous incumbent Robert Nixon (q.v.) as resident engineer. In 1834 Barry was listed as the piermaster for Scarborough Harbour.

William Barry died on Friday the 19th of October 1838 at his residence, Grove Villa, Scarborough, aged 55 years his obituary describing him as 'engineer to the Commissioners of Scarborough Piers'.

References - (29), (36a), (85f), (93), (95), (114).

BARRY, William   Scarborough architect & builder
1828 (Scarborough) - 1898 (Scarborough)

Scarborough work - Elder Street Dispensary (1858, demolished 1978), Cottage Hospital, Spring Hill Road (1870).

William Barry was the eldest son of Scarborough architect and building contractor John Barry (1803-66 q.v.) and trained with his father. As a young boy William Barry worked with Sir Samuel Morton Peto building railways in Norfolk and Suffolk. In the late 1840s William Barry joined his father and brother John (1833-1910 q.v.) in Scotland where his father had a contract to build the Victoria Dock at Leith. William Barry was left to supervise the work and it was in Leith that his first son, Frederick William, was born in 1851.

William Barry returned to Scarborough and was appointed surveyor to the Scarborough Improvement Commissioners in 1853 after the death of John Irvin (q.v.). Barry was also listed in Scarborough directories in the 1850s as an architect and he designed the Dispensary in Elder Street (opened 1858) and the Cottage Hospital for Mrs Anne Wright (1870). Among other buildings he was responsible for are Hadow (Haddo) Terrace in Aberdeen Walk and Royal Crescent, his own home being Royal Crescent Lodge.

William Barry was a partner in his father's brick, tile and terracotta manufacturing business at Barry's Lane on Seamer Road. After their father's death, John continued as a building contractor while William ran the manufacturing business, which in 1871 employed 33 men and 14 boys. Later he leased out the business.

As his father before him, William Barry was Mayor of Scarborough (1882-1883). He was a member of the Board of several Scarborough charities and became a Justice of the Peace in 1890. In 1885 he gave land for the enlargement of the Rotunda Museum.

William Barry's elder son Dr Frederick William Barry died suddenly in Birmingham 21st October 1897 aged 46 and William's wife Selina died 3 months later. Broken by these two deaths William died suddenly at his home on the 7th April 1898.

References – (14), (36a), (51), (85j), (94).

BARRY, William Ernest   **Scarborough & Hull architect**
1867 (Scarborough) - 1924 (Poole)

Scarborough work - Cottage Hospital, Spring Hill- new wing (1895-97), public conveniences at Scarborough Cemetery (1898).
see "Barry & Tugwell" and "Runton & Barry"

William Ernest Barry was the son of builder John Barry (1833-1910 q.v.) and was educated privately at Wharfedale College, Yorkshire. He worked with his father until 1882 when he became a pupil of the architect J.L. Clemence (q.v.) in Lowestoft until 1887. He then worked for 3 years with the firm of "George and Peto" (Sir Ernest George 1839-1922 & Harold Ainsworth Peto 1854-1933). Barry became an Associate of the Royal Institute of British Architects in 1892 his proposer being J.L.Clemence.

W.E.Barry returned to Scarborough where he had an independent practice from about 1895 about 1900. Barry's domestic work included alterations to a house for the Dowager Lady Cayley and his industrial work included alterations to factories in Melrose Street. Barry worked for the Scarborough Burial Board and also drew up plans for additions and a new wing for the Cottage Hospital in Spring Hill Road, which had been built in 1870 by his uncle William Barry (1828-98 q.v.).

W.E.Barry had a brief association with Frank Tugwell (q.v.) in 1897 and 1898 as "Barry & Tugwell' (q.v.). From about 1896 to 1918 Barry was in partnership with the Hull architect Percy Tom Runton as "Runton and Barry" (q.v.) with offices in Huntriss Row until 1910 when the Scarborough office closed. The Hull practice continued until about 1918 after which Barry moved his practice to Dorset.

William Ernest Barry died on the 17th July 1924 in Poole at the age of 56.

References – (14), (36a), (44), (86), (92c), (94), (101), (122), (123).

BARRY & TUGWELL   Scarborough architects' firm
William Ernest Barry (1867-1924)
Frank Tugwell (1862-1940)
fl.Sc. 1897-98

Scarborough work - alterations, additions and a new bakehouse for Scarborough Workhouse (1897-8).

William Ernest Barry (q.v.) and Frank Tugwell (q.v.) were briefly in partnership at 102, Westborough, Scarborough. In 1897 they entered two architectural competitions coming second in both. One was a design for a new College on Filey Road (won by "Hall, Cooper & Davis" q.v.) and the other for a new Wesleyan Chapel in Scarborough. During 1897 and 1898 "Barry & Tugwell" submitted plans on behalf of the Poor Law Guardians for alterations and additions to the Scarborough Workhouse.

References - (57), (94).

BEARD, Edwin Thomas   civil engineer
1861 (Lincoln) - post 1905
Scarborough work - Marine Drive (1900-1905).

Scarborough's Marine Drive was opened in 1908 after a construction period of 11 years. Edwin Thomas Beard was the resident engineer for the period 1900-1905.

Edwin Beard had been a pupil of the City Engineer of Lincoln and from 1887 his work involved a range of civil engineering work. This included sewerage, water supply, roads, bridges and in particular sea defence work along the south and south-east coast of England. Immediately before taking up his post at Scarborough, Beard was involved with sea defence works at Eastbourne and other projects.

References – (14), (36a), (61), (85k).

BEDFORD & KITSON   Leeds architects' firm
Bedford Francis William 1866 (Leeds) -1904
Kitson Sydney Decimus 1871 (Leeds) – 1937
fl. 1897-1903
Scarborough work – "Red Court", Esplanade (1900).
See also Sydney Kitson

"Bedford & Kitson" were in partnership in Leeds from 1897 to 1903 when
Francis Bedford moved to London.
In 1900 the firm designed a residence for a Leeds business man, Colonel
Frederick W.Tannett-Walker, at the south end of Esplanade known as "Red
Court".
References – (14), (18), (36a), (44), (46), (94).

BIRCH, Eugenius   civil engineer
1818 (Middlesex) - 1884 (London)

Scarborough work - North Bay Pier (1869, destroyed 1905), People's
Palace & Aquarium (1875, demolished 1966) and engineer to the
Scarborough to Whitby and to the Forge Valley Railway lines (1865-72).

Eugenius Birch was the son of an architect and surveyor and his talent for
engineering was apparent from an early age. He won a Silver Isis Medal
from the Society of Arts at the age of 19 for a drawing of a marine steam
engine and was elected a graduate of the Institution of Civil Engineers at
the age of 21. He entered partnership with his brother, John, doing much
railway work including the East Indian Railway from Calcutta to Delhi.
However, Eugenius Birch is remembered mostly for his seaside promenade
piers which he and his brother pioneered. The first they erected was at
Margate but this new feature of the town was not to everyone's taste, as
'The Builder' commented in 1855 "Whatever may be its (the Margate Pier)
mechanical sufficiency the ugliness of the new pier is unquestionable".
Other promenade piers followed and in 1864 the Scarborough Promenade
Pier Co. Ltd was formed to build the North Bay Pier to Birch's plans and
under his supervision. The partially completed Pier was opened in August
1868 and completed the next season. It was destroyed by a storm in 1905.
Having designed the aquarium at Brighton, a further attraction designed by
Eugenius Birch for Scarborough was the People's Palace and Aquarium
built in 1875 with huge sea water fish tanks.
Birch's railway expertise was also utilised locally as he was the first
engineer to the Scarborough to Whitby railway line which began operations
in 1865 but closed the next year because of depression in the North of
England. Birch was again involved as engineer producing plans for a new

route for the line in 1871 but work was slow because of lack of money and stopped in 1877, later continuing with other engineers. Birch also drew up plans for the associated Forge Valley line in 1872 which opened in 1882. Eugenius Birch died on the 8th of January 1884 at Hampstead after a long and painful illness.

References – (14), (15), (18), (38), (64), (70), (71), (85j), (89), (90).

BLACKETT, Thomas Oswald   **harbour surveyor**
- d. 1847 (Prudhoe)
Scarborough work - harbour works (1821-22).

Thomas Blackett, a member of a North East coal mining family, specialised in land, mining and engineering surveying. He was particularly involved with railway surveys including that of the Liverpool and Manchester Railway.
Blackett surveyed Scarborough Harbour for the engineer William Chapman (q.v.) and in 1821 published a plan of the harbour showing part of the town. In Scarborough Library there is a plan of William Chapman's proposed improvements to the Harbour (627.2.33) dated 1831 based on surveys by Blackett and John Barry (q.v.).
Thomas Blackett died following an accident on the Newcastle to Carlisle Railway in December 1847.

References – (65), (85h), (85i), (93), (114).

BODLEY, George Frederick   **London architect**
1827(Hull) - 1907 (Water Eaton, Oxon.)

Scarborough work - St Martin's-on-the-Hill Church, Albion Rd (1863), St Martin's Vicarage (1868), All Saints' Church, Falsgrave Rd (1868, demolished 1975), St Martin's Grammar School, Ramshill Rd (1872, closed 1922), enlargement of St Martin's Church (1879), St Michael's Church, Wheatcroft (1880).

George Bodley studied with the architect Sir George Gilbert Scott (1811-78) from 1845 to 1856, being his first pupil. Bodley travelled in France, Germany and Italy studying architecture and started his own professional practice in London in 1856, specialising in ecclesiastical work. He was superintendent of architecture at York Minster and Peterborough and Southwark Cathedrals, also working at many other cathedrals. From 1869 to 1897 he was in partnership with another pupil of Scott - Thomas Garner (1839-1906). Bodley became a fellow of the Royal Institute of British Architects in 1899, the same year that he received the Institute's Royal Gold Medal. He exhibited his architectural drawings at the Royal

13

Academy on many occasions between 1854 and 1904 and was elected to the Academy in 1902. He is best known for his church work, which included furnishings and monuments such as that to the dead of the Boer War (1905) in York.

In Scarborough Bodley's main work is St Martin's-on-the-Hill, consecrated in July 1863. He was responsible for all later additions to the Church including a vestry and sacristry (1869), enlargements (1879), the reredos (1890) and extensions to the north aisle chapel (1902). Bodley also designed a parsonage for St Martin's Church (1868) and St Martin's Grammar School (1872). Two further Scarborough churches by Bodley were All Saints' Church in Falsgrave (1868) and St Michael's Church at Wheatcroft which was built as a mission church for the area known as 'New Brighton'.

Elsewhere in the country Bodley was prolific and he continued working until his death. He died on the 21st October 1907, aged 80 having that year drawn up plans for a new vestry for St Martin's Church in Scarborough and was in the midst of preparing plans for a cathedral at San Francisco .

References - (14), (18), (21), (25), (30), (44), (46), (50), (54), (57), (85j), (85k), (92a), (92b), (92c), (94), (99), (101), (102), (104), (106).

BRERETON, Cuthbert Arthur   **civil engineer**
1851 (Norfolk) - 1910 (Twickenham)

Scarborough work - (associated with) Marine Drive (1900).

Scarborough's Marine Drive was opened in 1908 after a construction period of 11 years. An article in the Scarborough Mercury listed the engineers associated with the project and included Cuthbert Brereton who was consulted in 1900.

Cuthbert Brereton's early engineering work was with a series of railway companies. In 1880 he became a member of the Institution of Civil Engineers and from 1893 to 1909 he was in partnership with Sir John Wolfe Barry in London. The partnership was involved with a range of dock construction projects including those at Barry, Middlesborough, Surrey and Hull. It was during this period of his career that Brereton was consulted on Marine Drive then under construction.

References – (14), (64), (85k).

BRIERLEY, Walter Henry   Yorkshire architect
1862 (Lowton, Lancs.) - 1926

Scarborough work - "Brackencliffe", Esplanade Crescent (1905).

Walter Brierley was articled to his father Richard (b.1838) and in 1885 entered into partnership in York with James Demaine (q.v.) as "Demaine & Brierley" (q.v.)

In 1901 Walter Brierley was appointed architect to the North Riding County Council, an appointment he held until his resignation in 1923. He designed the County Buildings in Northallerton (1906) and was responsible for maintaining all County Council buildings although he continued his private practice and designed a number of large residences in the county.

In Scarborough, Walter Brierley designed a villa, "Brackencliffe", for the York born surgeon/dentist Walter Glaisby (1905). In 1914 Brierley drew up plans a new church hall for St Saviour's Church and at nearby Hackness he restored the interior of Hackness Hall after a fire in 1910.

Walter H.Brierley, FSA FRIBA died in 1926

References – (14), (18), (36a), (44), (46), (54), (57), (92a), (92b), (92c), (94), (101), (122).

BRODRICK, Cuthbert   Hull, Leeds & London architect
1822 (Hull) - 1905 (Jersey)

Scarborough work - Grand Hotel (1867).

Cuthbert Brodrick was articled to architect H.F.Lockwood (1811-78 q.v.) until 1843, the following year making an architectural tour of Europe, including France and Italy. He refused a partnership with Lockwood and set up on his own in Hull but later practised from Leeds and London. He was elected Fellow of the Royal Institute of British Architects in 1860.

Amongst his Yorkshire buildings are Leeds Town Hall (1853-8), Leeds Corn Exchange (1861), Leeds Mechanics' Institute (1865-8 later the Civic Theatre) and Leeds Congregational Church, Headingly Lane (1864-6). In Hull he designed the Town Hall (1861) which was demolished and replaced by the present Guildhall of 1906-14 (by Edwin Cooper q.v.) using some material from the Town Hall. Brodrick built a hotel in Withernsea (1854) which later became the hospital and also in Yorkshire restored churches and designed some vicarages. In 1854 he exhibited his design for Leeds Town Hall at the Royal Academy, and the following year a design for the Ilkley Hydropathic Establishment.

Brodrick submitted two unsuccessful designs in Scarborough, one for a new font in St Mary's Church (1860) and one for the church of St Martin'son-the-Hill (1861) which was built to the plans of fellow Hull architect George F.Bodley (q.v.).

Brodrick's design for Scarborough's Grand Hotel was described as the climax of the English use of the French "Second Empire" style. Brodrick had studied this in Paris in the early 1850s at the time of its rebuilding by Baron Haussmann (1809-91). The building of the hotel was fraught with difficulties because of its site on St Nicholas' Cliff which required extensive sub-structural work. Added to this was the failure of the initial contractor Daniel Climie (q.v.) when the building was only half built and the bankruptcy of the initial developer, the Scarborough Cliff Hotel Co., in 1865. It was, however, completed and finally opened as the Grand Hotel on the 24th July 1867, in which year Brodrick exhibited his design of the Grand Hotel at the Royal Academy in London. It has been suggested that, while in Scarborough, Brodrick was inspired by Josiah Fairbank's (q.v.) design for the Moorish Public Baths at Bland's Cliff to use a similar design for his oriental baths in Leeds (1866).

The Grand Hotel, Scarborough was to be Brodrick's last major building. It is said that he felt humiliated when his design for Manchester Town Hall was turned down, and from about 1870 he lived in Paris where he is reputed to have worked as a penniless waiter. He did no further architectural work after 1875 living in obscurity in France. His last years were spent in Jersey where he died on the 2nd of March 1905.

References - (18), (44), (46), (54), (57), (74), (84), (85j), (92a), (92b), (92c), (101), (102), (106).

BROWN, William Raffles   **Liverpool architect**
fl.Sc. 1850

Scarborough work - Bar Congregational Church, Westborough 1850 (demolished 1962).

In 1849 a committee under the chairmanship of Sir William Lowthrop was formed with the object of building a new independent chapel in Scarborough. Each member was asked to approach an architect for a design and six were received including one from John Petch of Scarborough (1819-97 q.v.). The design by William Raffles Brown of Liverpool was chosen and the Bar Church in Westborough was opened in August 1850. William Raffles Brown was a nephew of the Rev. Dr Thomas Raffles (1788-1863) an independent Liverpool minister who preached the sermon at the formal opening of the Bar Church. Raffles Brown designed several churches in the Liverpool area between 1848 and 1853 but appears to have moved to London by 1854.

References – (54), (57), (85j), (90), (92e), (92k), (101).

BURGESS, Edward   London architect
fl.Sc 1881-82.

Scarborough work – "Wrea Head", Scalby near Scarborough (1881),
"Messrs W. Rowntree, Sons & Co." department store, Westborough (1882,
demolished 1990).

Edward Burgess designed William Rowntree's Scarborough Department
Store at 33-39, Westborough which opened in 1882. This later became
Debenham's Stores and was demolished in 1990 to make way for the
Brunswick Centre. Burgess not only designed the building but personally
supervised its construction and for a period of time the clerk of works was
his pupil Fred Rowntree (q.v.). Also in 1882 Burgess drew up plans for
additions to Lady Sitwell's Scarborough house, "Woodend".
In Scalby, near Scarborough, Burgess designed a house known as "Wrea
Head" for the liberal MP, John Edward Ellis.
Edward Burgess exhibited some of his architectural drawings at the Royal
Academy between 1880 and 1888, including "New Premises,
Scarborough" (Rowntree's Store) in 1885 and "Wrea Head near
Scarborough" in 1886.
References – (46), (54), (85j), (85k), (94), (119).

BURY, Charles Augustus   Scarborough architect
1846 (Lincoln) - post 1885

Scarborough work - Christ Church, Vernon Place, restoration (1873,
demolished 1979), Unitarian Church, Falsgrave Rd (1876), St Paul's
Mission and Coffee House, Regent St, (1879), St Nicholas Cliff Tramway
(1881), Vernon Place Baths, later the Art School (1883 destroyed 1941),
"Daily Post" Offices, Huntriss Row (1883) "Lynwood", 16, Filey Rd
(1883).

Charles Augustus Bury was an assistant to W.B.Stewart (q.v.) and entered
into partnership with him about 1870 as "Stewart & Bury" (q.v.) but the
partnership was dissolved the following year.
Charles Bury then worked independently until the early 1880s and was
company architect to Scarborough Spa producing many designs, none of
which were ever executed. They included a skating rink, conservatories,
picture galleries, billiard halls and refreshment rooms, baths and a winter
garden. Within a month of the fire that destroyed the Spa in 1876 Bury had
produced plans for its restoration at a cost of £6,000, but the commission
went to "Verity and Hunt" (q.v.). Bury submitted a bill of over £1,216 for
his efforts but was paid only £700. A further Bury project that was never

realised was his plan for a road bridge linking St Nicholas' Cliff to South Cliff argued on the grounds that Valley Bridge was too remote from the (then) town centre (1873).

Charles Bury had a major domestic practice in Scarborough but was also responsible for much public work. He planned the restoration of Christ Church, Vernon Place in 1873 (built 1828 by Atkinson q.v.) which involved re-seating and re-flooring and a new parish room. He designed the Unitarian Church on Falsgrave Road (1876) and St Paul's Mission House, Regent Street, which included a coffee and refreshment house to attract people to the church (1879). His secular work varied from rebuilding the 'Post Office Tavern' in Merchants' Row (1880) to offices in Huntriss Row for the 'Daily Post' Company and the Vernon Place Baths, built for the 'Sanatorium and Medical Bath Company Ltd' which were converted for use as Scarborough Art School in 1884 by John Hall (q.v.). He also designed "Lynwood" on Filey Road for Mr Thompson Allen.

Charles Bury completed the new Primitive Methodist Church in St John's Road, Falsgrave which had been designed by one of his pupils, Godfrey Peacock (q.v.) who had died before the project was finished. Further pupils were Henry Hare (q.v.) who became President of the Royal Institute of British Architects, Thomas Davison (q.v.) both these students winning the prestigious Ashpitel prize of the Royal Institute of British Architects in 1886 and 1887 respectively and Fred Rowntree (q.v.).

At the beginning of the 1880s Bury also had a practice in Rhyl, where he designed several houses, including one for his father in law, Archibald Fuller, a retired East India Merchant. However, in 1884 Charles Bury was adjudged bankrupt and moved to London shortly afterwards.

References - (14), (36a), (44), (49), (85j), (85k), (94), (118), (120).

CARROLL, Joseph Henry   **Scarborough architect**
1839 (Ireland) - post 1897

Scarborough work - none known

Joseph Carroll is listed under 'architects' in Scarborough directories between 1883 and 1890, describing himself as 'architect to Lord Londesborough' in the 1887 edition. By 1897 he had moved to West Ayton, near Scarborough.

A newspaper report of 1881 named the architect to the Seamer (near Scarborough) School Board as 'Mr Carrall' - probably Joseph Carroll. The Seamer and Irton Board School had been erected in 1878.

In East Yorkshire J.H.Carroll extended a large mansion in Londesborough Park (1875) and in 1877 designed a school and master's house at Skerne.

References - (23), (36a), (85j), (92c).

18

CHAMBERS, William   Scarborough architect
fl.Sc 1822-23

Scarborough work - none known

Scarborough directories for 1822 and 1823 list William Chambers as an architect of Long Westgate. The same directories also list a William Chambers junior as a stone mason.
References - (36a), (92c).

CHAPMAN, Henry Ascough   Scarborough & Leeds architect
1873 (Scarborough) - 1939 (Bexhill-on-Sea)

Scarborough work - Dr Horne's Homes, Londesborough Rd (1908).

Henry Chapman, son of a chemist and druggist in the town, was articled to the Scarborough architect J.Caleb Petch (q.v.) from 1889 to 1894. Over the same period Chapman attended Scarborough School of Art where, among other prizes, he was awarded one for architectural drawing in 1895. In the same year he became an Associate of the Royal Institute of British Architects, becoming a Fellow in 1909.
H. A. Chapman practised independently in Scarborough from 1899 to 1909 initially in Huntriss Row and later in Westborough and also had offices in Leeds. Besides domestic work, Chapman drew up plans in 1900 to convert the New Empire Building on Foreshore to Municipal Swimming Baths which were described in great detail in the local newspaper (but were never built) He designed Dr John Horne's Homes in Londesborough Road (1908). Chapman left Scarborough to live in Bexhill-on-Sea and in 1913 was appointed housing inspector for the Ministry of Health, an appointment he held until 1934.
Henry Ascough Chapman died on the 8th January 1939.
References - (14), (36a), (44), (54), (85j), (94), (100), (101), (122), (123), (124).

CHAPMAN, William   civil engineer
1749 (Whitby) - 1832

Scarborough work – Scalby Sea Cut, (1804), consulting engineer for Scarborough Harbour (1800-31).

William Chapman trained as a civil engineer, obtaining appointments in Ireland with the Grand Canal and the Kildare Canal. While working on the latter Chapman developed the 'skew arch' bridge which allowed the canal to be crossed at an oblique angle in order that the continuity of the road might be preserved. This architectural device became widely adopted.

Chapman returned to Newcastle Upon Tyne where, with his brother, he ran the family rope works, inventing and patenting several machines for improvements.

Chapman, who was also associated with bridge building in Newcastle, was involved with Sir John Rennie designing the London Dock and the South Dock & Basin at Hull. Chapman also did harbour work at Seaham and was engineer to Commissioners of Leith Harbour.

In Scarborough William Chapman was engineer to the Harbour Commissioners from 1800 to 1831 and superintended all ongoing work. He produced a series of reports on the state of the harbour during his tenure together with proposals for improvements. Scarborough Library hold a plan, dated 1831, of William Chapman's proposed improvements drawn up from surveys done by T.O.Blackett (q.v.) and John Barry (q.v.).

Also in the Scarborough area William Chapman was responsible for drawing up plans to drain the upper Derwent Valley which resulted in building the 'Sea Cut' from Everley to the sea at Scalby Mills (opened 3rd September 1804).

William Chapman died on the 19th May, 1832, aged 83.

References - (17), (26), (35), (63), (65), (85k), (85m), (92c), (93), (95), (99), (114).

CHEERS, Henry Arthur   **London architect**
1853 (Chester) - post 1895

Scarborough work - Constitutional Club (now the Conservative Club), Huntriss Row (1888).

Henry Cheers entered many architectural competitions between 1883 and 1900 particularly for public buildings. In 1887 he submitted a design for a new building for The Scarborough Constitutional Club Company Ltd. At its first meeting of shareholders in September 1887, with Lord Londesborough in chair, the directors chose the plans of Henry Cheers from the 90 submitted. The foundation stone was laid in January 1888 and the building was opened in December 1888 by the Prime Minister, the Marquis of Salisbury.

Elsewhere in Yorkshire Henry Cheers designed a Library and School of Art in Doncaster (1888 - now demolished), the Northern Library in Hull (1895) and a new wing for Harlow Manor Hydro, Harrogate (1893).

References - (14), (46), (57), (85j), (92a), (92b), (92c), (94), (101).

CHRISTIAN, Ewan   **London architect**
1814 (Marylebone) - 1895 (Hampstead)

Scarborough work - Restoration of St Mary's Parish Church (1848-1852), National Schools, Queen St (1859), Holy Trinity Church, Westbourne Grove (1880).

Ewan Christian was a pupil of the architect Matthew Habershon (1789-1852) and later of John Brown (d.1876) and also studied at the Royal Academy Schools. After travelling on the Continent, Christian set up in practice in London in 1842. From 1847 he was consulting architect to both Lichfield and Carlisle Diocesan Societies and to the Ecclesiastical Commissioners. He was one of the most prominent and prolific ecclesiastical architects of his generation, active until his death in 1895. He became an Associate of the Royal Institute of British Architects in 1840, a Fellow in 1850 and was President from 1884 to 1886.
In Scarborough, in 1847, Ewan Christian successfully competed for the restoration the Parish Church of St Mary. In 1848 he exhibited drawings of his work at St Mary's at the Royal Academy in London, this being one of Christian's earliest church restorations. In 1859, Scarborough National Schools were demolished and a new building designed by Ewan Christian was erected. Christian also designed Holy Trinity Church, Scarborough, consecrated in 1880.
Ewan Christian died, aged 80, on the 21st of February 1895.
References - (14), (18), (21), (25), (26), (44), (46), (50), (54), (57), (60), (85j), (92a), (92c), (101), (102), (104), (111).

CLARK, Edwin   **London civil engineer**
1814 - 1894 (Marlow)

Scarborough work - (Ramsdale) Valley Bridge (consulted 1862).

Edwin Clark was experienced in bridge construction having been resident engineer during the building of Robert Stephenson's Bridges, the Britannia Bridge at Menai and the Conway Tubular Bridge and had written a two volume book about their construction. Clarke was also responsible for the Anderton Boat Lift in Northwich, Cheshire.
In Scarborough a scheme to build a bridge across Ramsdale Valley had been mooted as early as 1848 and received Town Council approval but on conditions that deterred any company from progressing with the project. Such a bridge was again proposed in 1862 by Robert Williamson, Chairman of the "York City & County Bank" and a director of North Eastern Railway, who had bought a skeleton iron bridge which had

collapsed into the River Ouse at York. There was again much controversy and debate in the town, the main justification being that a bridge would open up the area south of the valley, known as the Weaponess Estate, for a development such as that proposed by Sir Joseph Paxton (q.v.). The Town Council commissioned a report from Edwin Clark which was favourable and in spite of two further years of debate the Scarborough Valley Bridge Company Act received its Royal assent in June 1864. The iron work from the Ouse Bridge formed the basis of Scarborough's Valley Bridge which was opened in July 1865.

Edwin Clark died on the 22nd of October 1894 after many years involvement with all aspects of civil engineering including railways here and abroad.

References – (18), (64), (85j), (108).

CLEMENCE, John Louth   Lowestoft architect
1822 - 1911 (Lowestoft)

Scarborough work - superintended work for Henry Wyatt.

John Clemence was pupil of the architect Charles Robert Cockerell (1788-1863) in London from 1839 to 1843.

In Scarborough, in 1843, Clemence superintended work for Henry Wyatt (q.v.), probably at The Spa.

Clemence later set up practice as an architect in Lowestoft and between 1882 and 1887 William Ernest Barry (q.v.) was one of his pupils.

References - (44).

CLIMIE Daniel   Shrewsbury civil engineer & contractor
1815 (Scotland) - post 1868

Scarborough work - initial contractor for Scarborough Cliff (Grand) Hotel (1863).

Daniel Climie was established by 1851 as a civil engineer, contractor and proprietor of a brick making works in Shrewsbury.

In 1862 the Scarborough Cliff Hotel Company had been formed to build a large hotel designed by Cuthbert Brodrick (q.v.). Daniel Climie won the building contract and work began in June 1863. However, when the building was only two floors high on the land side and five on the sea side, Climie defaulted on the contract and the Company was wound up in 1865. A new company was formed and Scarborough's 'Grand Hotel' was completed by another contractor, Archibald Neill of Bradford.

In January 1864 it was announced that Daniel Climie was the successful contractor for the proposed railway from Scarborough to Whitby although by 1865 a Mr Tredwell was stated to be the contractor, presumably because of Climie's failure at the Grand Hotel. Also in 1864 a Mr R. (sic) Climie, civil engineer, presumably Daniel, wrote to the Scarborough Gazette arguing the case for a tramway from Scarborough to Cloughton via Falsgrave, with a breakdown of the costs. This was never built.

Daniel Climie continued to submit (unsuccessful) tenders for building work in Scarborough including for All Saints Church (1867) and for an extension to the west pier at Scarborough Harbour (1868). Tenders for this harbour work were also submitted by James Austin (q.v.) who shared a business address with Climie in Scarborough (120, North Marine Road) and who had been associated with him in Shrewsbury.

References – (14), (36a), (61), (70), (85j).

COODE, Sir John W.   **London civil engineer**
1816 (Bodmin) - 1892 (Brighton)

Scarborough work - (consulted 1882-89 on plans for) Royal Albert Drive and Marine Drive.

John Coode set up in practice as a civil engineer in London in 1844 after gaining experience in the construction of the Great Western and Bristol Railway. He was resident engineer at Portland Harbour from 1844 to 1872 and shortly after the completion of this work received a knighthood. In 1858 he was appointed a member of the Royal Commission on Harbours of Refuge and inspected more than 30 important harbours Britain. In the same year he examined Filey Bay and stressed its importance geographically and naturally and pointed out its exceptional advantages as a military and strategic harbour. The harbour was never built but as late as 1875 Coode was still arguing the case for Filey.

In 1882 Scarborough Corporation approached Sir John Coode, by now one of the most eminent and experienced harbour engineers consulted by Governments around the world. Coode was asked to give an opinion on a proposed road under Castle Cliff to join north and south bays. Coode prepared a series of reports between 1882 and 1889 which supported the construction of Royal Albert Drive, opened in 1890 and Marine Drive, begun five years after his death, and only completed in 1908.

Sir John Coode died on the 2nd of March 1892.

References - (18), (43), (64), (85j), (85k), (99).

COOPER, Sir Thomas Edwin　　　　　　**London architect**
1874 (Scarborough) - 1942

Scarborough work - Alterations to Chemist's shop, Princess St for Mrs Williamson (1894), Tennis Pavilion, South Cliff (1910 & 1913), Spa Bandstand and cafe (1913), Additions to "Scarborough Mercury" Office and a store, Aberdeen Walk (1913).
see also "Cooper & Davis", "Hall, Cooper & Davis" and "Russell & Cooper".

Thomas Edwin Cooper, son of a cab proprietor, Samuel Cooper, became a pupil of the Scarborough architects' firm "Hall & Tugwell" (q.v.). He later went to London to work in the office of "Goldie, Child & Goldie" who specialised in the design of Roman Catholic Churches. Cooper returned to Scarborough about 1896/7 and joined John Hall (q.v.) and Herbert Davis (q.v.) to form the partnership "Hall, Cooper & Davis" (q.v.) which lasted until about 1902.
The following year the partnership became "Cooper & Davis" (q.v.) on the departure of John Hall. By 1905 Cooper was working only from his London Office, having become a Fellow of the Royal Institute of British Architects in 1903, Herbert Davis having set up an independent practice in Scarborough. Cooper was then in partnership with Samuel Bridgman Russell until 1912 as "Russell & Cooper" (q.v.).
Even though established in London, Cooper maintained his contact with Scarborough. He drew up plans for a pavilion for the Lawn Tennis Club (1910 /13), alterations and additions to the Spa including the bandstand and cafe (1913) and modifications to the "Scarborough Mercury" Office for Meredith T.Whittaker (1913).
After 1912 Cooper styled himself 'T.Edwin Cooper', and his work was mainly in London. One of his earliest buildings was for the Port of London Authority, in Trinity Square (1912-22) described by Sir Nikolaus Pevsner as "a lasting monument to Edwardian optimism, like a super-palace for an International Exhibition, showy, happily vulgar and extremely impressive".
Cooper was knighted in 1923 and he exhibited his architectural designs extensively at the Royal Academy until his death, being elected a Royal Academician in 1937.
Sir Edwin Cooper died on the 24th of June 1942.
References - (14), (18), (19), (36a), (44), (46), (74), (85k), (92c), (94), (96), (100), (101), (118), (122), (123), (124).

COOPER & DAVIS   **Scarborough architects' firm**
Thomas Edwin Cooper (1874 - 1942)
Herbert Davis (1872 -)
fl. 1903-1905

Scarborough work - domestic.

The Scarborough firm of "Cooper & Davis" came into being in 1903 when John Hall (q.v.) left the firm of "Hall, Cooper & Davis" (q.v.). Between 1903 and 1905 "Cooper & Davis" did mainly domestic work including drawing up plans for 19 houses on the Belle Vue Estate in Scarborough in 1903. In the same year the partners exhibited (from a London address) three architectural drawings at the Royal Academy including one entitled "House at Scarborough".
References – (54), (92c), (94).

CROSBY, Thomas Wrangles   **Scarborough architect and surveyor**
fl.Sc 1855-1879

Scarborough work - domestic.

Thomas W.Crosby was listed as "joiner & undertaker, patentee of the newly invented bathing machine" in the 1855 directory at 5, Auborough Street. By 1867 he is listed as an architect (and bathing machine owner) of 5, Hoxton Road, Scarborough. The 1879 directory lists Thomas Crosby as an architect and surveyor of 15, Barwick Street and in the same year he prepared plans for houses and a joiner's shop in Durham Street, and a wooden auction mart in Castle Road. No patent in Crosby's name has been traced.
References – (36a), (94).

CROZIER, William   **civil engineer**
1830 (Co, Durham) - post 1902

Scarborough work - none known

William Crozier, a member of the Institution of Civil Engineers, was listed in Scarborough street indexes but not trade lists from 1890 to 1902, perhaps suggesting he had retired to the town. He had previously been engineer for the Borough of Sunderland and later engineer to the County of Durham
References – (14), (36a), (62).

DAVIS, Edward   **Scarborough civil engineer**
1839 (Whitmore, Staffs.) - post 1890

Scarborough work – clerk of works, Scarborough Water Works (1880s).

Edward Davis was clerk of works for the building of Scarborough Waterwork's new plant at Irton and for a new reservoir on Oliver's Mount. The consulting engineer for the project was Edward Filliter (q.v.) and the resident engineer William Millhouse (q.v.). The waterworks were opened in 1881.
References – (14), (36a).

DAVIS, Herbert   **Scarborough architect**
1872 (Essex) - post 1913

Scarborough work – alterations to Scarborough Rowing Club premises (1891).
see "Hall, Cooper & Davis", "Cooper & Davis" and "Davis & Baker".

Herbert Davis, son of the civil engineer Edward Davis (q.v.), attended Scarborough School of Art where he was amongst the prize winning students between 1890 and 1894. While still a student he drew up plans for alterations to Scarborough Rowing Club (1891). From about 1896 to 1904 he was a member of the firms of "Hall, Cooper & Davis" (q.v.) and "Cooper & Davis" (q.v.).
In 1904 Herbert Davis became a Fellow of the Royal Institute of British Architects and set up an independent practice at 7, York Place, Scarborough but the following year he took Frank Baker (q.v.) into partnership as "Davis & Baker" (q.v.) until 1913 after which only Baker is listed at this address.
References - (14), (36a), (85j), (94), (101).

DAVIS & BAKER   **Scarborough architects' firm**
fl. 1905-1913
Herbert Davis (1872 - post 1913)
Frank Baker

Scarborough work - Theatre in Queen St (1906), alterations to St Mary's School, Castle Rd (1908), covered stand for Scarborough Cricket Club (1910).

Herbert Davis (q.v.) formed a partnership with Frank Baker (q.v) about

1904 to form the firm of "Davis & Baker" which continued until about 1913. The firm's work was mainly domestic although they drew up plans for a theatre in Queen Street for Joseph Scott of the Castle Hotel (1906), alterations to St Mary's School, Castle Road (1908) and a covered stand for Scarborough Cricket Club (1910).

References – (36a), (94).

DAVISON, Thomas   **Scarborough architect & builder**
1800 (Scarborough) - 1862 (Scarborough)

Scarborough work - St Thomas' Church, East Sandgate (1840).

Thomas Davison carried on business as a builder and joiner in the town from at least 1834 until his death in 1862. He was the architect for St Thomas's Church, East Sandgate, the foundation stone for which was laid on St Thomas's Day (21st December) 1839 and which was opened exactly one year later in 1840.

References - (14), (36a), (85k), (85m), (104), (114).

DAVISON, Thomas   **London architect**
1864 (Scarborough) - post 1914

Scarborough work - small domestic.

Thomas Davison, the son of a local baker, was articled to the Scarborough architect Charles A.Bury (q.v.) for four years. Davison worked briefly in Scarborough in 1885/6 with small domestic projects after which he moved to London as an assistant in various offices and studied at the Royal Academy Schools. In 1887 he won the Ashpitel Prize of the Royal Institute of British Architects, the year after Henry Hare (q.v.), another of Bury's pupils, had also won this prestigious award. In 1888 Davison became an Associate of the Royal Institute of British Architects and continued practising in London where he was associated for a time with Hare. In 1897 the two architects signed a letter to 'The Builder' defending a design for an extension to Liverpool Museum. Davison was living in Purley in 1914.

References - (14), (18), (44), (54), (57), (94), (101), (122).

DEMAINE, James   York architect
1843 (Yorks.) - post 1902

Scarborough work – "Netherbank" and "Shortlands", Filey Rd (1883).

James Demaine designed two villas on Filey Road, in Scarborough in 1883, "Netherbank" for businessman John Dale and "Shortlands" for a Miss Hood.

James Demaine took Walter Brierley (q.v.) into practice as "Demaine & Brierley" (q.v.) about 1885.

References – (14), (92c), (94).

DEMAINE & BRIERLEY   York architects' firm
James Demaine (1843 -)
Walter Brierley (1862-1926)
fl. 1885 - 1902

Scarborough work - alterations to Beckett's bank, St Nicholas' St (1899), Holy Trinity Memorial Hall (1902).

In 1885 James Demaine (q.v.) took Walter Brierley (q.v.) into partnership in York as "Demaine & Brierley" the partnership lasting until 1902.

"Demaine & Brierley" entered several architectural competitions throughout the country including one for a bank in Whitby (1891 York City & Co. Banking Co. now HSBC) for which they were awarded first prize and one for Scarborough's Higher Grade school in 1897 in which they came second to "Hall, Cooper & Davis" (q.v.). They also exhibited several architectural designs at the Royal Academy between 1892 and 1897.

In Scarborough "Demaine & Brierley" designed alterations to 38 and 39, St Nicholas' Street, for Beckett's Bank (1899) and in 1902 they designed a memorial hall for Holy Trinity Church, Westbourne Grove to commemorate the death of Queen Victoria.

References – (57), (92a), (92b), (92c), (94).

EDESON, Charles   **Scarborough architect**
1851 (York) - post 1914

Scarborough work - "Fairholme", 9, Valley Rd (1891), Scarborough Aquarium, - swimming baths (1893), Wesleyan Chapel and School at Seamer (1894), Scarborough Aquarium, - theatre (1895), Pavilion at Scarborough Cricket Club (1903).
see also "Edeson & Rowntree"

Charles Edeson began his architectural career in Scarborough in the early 1870s and continued in the town until about 1914. From about 1884 to 1889 he was in partnership with Fred Rowntree (q.v.) as "Edeson & Rowntree" (q.v.) although he also worked independently.
In Scarborough much of Charles Edeson's work was domestic including designs for houses, cottages and villas, but he also designed several industrial warehouses. Amongst his clients were "The Aquarium Company", for which he designed swimming baths in 1892, a new theatre in 1895 and a house known as "Fairholme" in Valley Road for the company's manager William Morgan in 1891. He also worked for The Royal Northern Sea Bathing Infirmary, Scarborough School Board and W Rowntree & Son. Edeson supervised the construction of St Saviour's Church, Gladstone Road, designed by J.T.Micklethwaite (q.v.). In 1903 Edeson designed a press and scorer pavilion for Scarborough Cricket Club and at nearby Seamer he designed a Wesleyan Chapel and adjacent school, opened in 1894.
Edeson & Son. From 1912-1914 Charles Edeson was in partnership with one of his sons as "Charles Edeson & Son". Edeson had two sons who became architects and the partnership was likely to have been with the younger son George as the elder, Charles A. had moved to Derbyshire by 1914.
George E.Edeson, born Scarborough 1882, also studied at Scarborough School of Art over the same period as his brother, also winning prizes. George E.Edeson is listed as an architect in the 1915 Scarborough directory but does not appear in later lists.
Charles Alva Edeson, born 1880 in Scarborough studied at Scarborough School of Art where he was amongst the prize winners between 1897 and 1900, one of his prizes being for a design for a town hall. In 1902 he drew up plans for Scarborough School Board for alterations to a cottage in Ackworth Street. He became an Associate of the Royal Institute of British Architects and moved to Normanton, Derbys. By 1923 he was working in the Borough Engineer's Office in Mansfield.
References - (14), (36a), (85j), (85k), (89), (94), (101), (122), (123), (124).

EDESON & ROWNTREE   **Scarborough architects' firm**
Charles Edeson (1851 -)
Fred Rowntree (1860 - 1927)
fl. 1884-90

Scarborough work - Warehouse, Wooler St (1884), villa - 50, Westbourne Park (1886), villa - "Endcliffe", Granville Rd (1888), Weaponness Estate plan (1889).

Charles Edeson (q.v.) and Fred Rowntree (q.v.) went into partnership in Scarborough about 1884 as "Edeson & Rowntree", the firm lasting until about 1890.

In Scarborough they designed a wide range of villas, houses and cottages including 50, Westbourne Park for William F.Wilkinson and a villa for William Stickney Rowntree – "Endcliffe", Granville Road. They also designed conversions and alterations for commercial properties and a warehouse and cottages in Wooler Street for "William Rowntree & Sons" (1884). In 1889 their plans for a layout for the Weaponness Estate won first prize of £150 out of eleven entries from around the country. Their layout was displayed to the public in Scarborough Town Hall.

References – (36a), (85j), (85k), (94).

ELIOT, Whately   **civil engineer**
fl.Sc. 1886-7

Scarborough work - Royal Albert Drive and North Cliff improvements (1886-7).

Whately Eliot was a pupil of Sir John Coode (q.v.) between 1861 and 1864 and went on to specialise in harbour, pier and associated work throughout England. He worked at Sunderland docks and later at Tynemouth pier where he was principle assistant to Philip Messent (q.v.). Coode chose Eliot as his assistant for other harbour works including those on the Isle of Man and in New Zealand.

In 1886 John Coode had been asked by Scarborough Council to draw up plans for a road around North Bay and to lay out and improve the North Cliff. The plans were modified by Joseph Petch (q.v.), the Borough Engineer, to reduce costs and Whately Eliot was appointed resident engineer for the project. Eliot drew up detailed constructional plans and sections, but resigned in 1887 to take up another post. However his account of this work was published in a paper entitled 'The North Seawall and Royal Albert Drive, Scarborough' in the Proceedings of the Institution of Civil Engineers (1890/1). Whately Eliot was replaced by Robert Aytoun

(q.v.) and Royal Albert Drive was formally opened by HRH the Duke of Clarence in June 1890. The foundation stone for Royal Albert Drive, laid with full Masonic honours by the Mayor John W.Woodall on the 1st of January 1887 bears Whately Eliot's name as engineer.
References – (61), (64), (85j), (85k).

EVERETT, John Edward   **civil engineer**
1859 - post 1900

Scarborough work - Marine Drive (1896-1900).

John Everett spent much of his working life involved with railway building projects in Ireland. In 1889 Sir John Coode (q.v.) had drawn up plans for a road under Castle Cliff to join Royal Albert Drive to Scarborough Harbour and in the mid 1890s John Everett was appointed to prepare detailed plans and specifications for the project. In March 1896 he was appointed resident engineer to direct the work, the foundation stone for which was laid in June 1897.
Everett continued in this post until June 1900 and Marine Drive was finally opened in August 1908.
References – (18), (61), (85j), (85k).

FAIRBANK, Josiah Forster   **Scarborough civil engineer**
1822 (Sheffield) - post 1878

Scarborough work - Engineer to Gasworks (1851), Public Baths, Bland's Cliff (1859), North Cliff Rock Gardens (1860).

Josiah Fairbank studied as a civil engineer and surveyor under his father in Sheffield. An early post was as resident engineer to the Pudsey Gas Works (near Leeds) for three years. He was appointed Engineer in Chief for Scarborough and other gas works in 1851 and was also engineer to Filey Water Works. On the basis of this experience he was elected a member of the Institution of Civil Engineers in 1857.
Also in Scarborough, he was engineer to the Public Bath Company in Scarborough and in 1858 he superintended the erection of new baths on the foreshore near Bland's Cliff. He was responsible for both the engineering aspects of the baths as well as their external appearance. His design was described by the Scarborough Gazette of the day as including ".. a lofty Mooresque water tower and dome besides a minareted chimney shaft". The building is presently an amusement arcade. It has been suggested that Fairbank's baths inspired Cuthbert Brodrick (q.v.), architect of Scarborough's Grand Hotel, to use a similar design for some oriental

baths in Leeds in 1866.

In 1860 Fairbank conceived a plan for a pedestrian tunnel, 540 yards long, to join Scarborough's North and South Bays. The plan was accepted by the Town Council but never carried out. Also in 1860, Fairbank laid out ornamental gardens and a wooden structure said to seat almost 2000 people on the North Cliff known as the Rock Gardens. However, because of engineering and other problems the scheme was not a success.

Fairbank moved to London in the early 1860s but still kept in contact with Scarborough. In 1865 he tried to revive his tunnel plan pointing out that the 540 yards tunnel would, for a small toll, obviate the 2,600 yards route over the hill, and that it would be wide enough to allow the lifeboat to be run through in 3 minutes if it was required urgently in North Bay. The tunnel plan was again revived in 1894 but never realised. In 1876 Fairbank prepared plans for improvements to Scarborough Harbour which, although approved by the Harbour Commissioners, were never carried out although Fairbank again wrote from London in 1878 to ask that these plans should be reconsidered.

References – (5), (14), (18), (36a), (62), (74), (85j), (94).

FILLITER, Edward　　　　　　　　　　　**Leeds civil engineer**
1826 (Dorset) - post 1881

Scarborough work - extension to Scarborough Waterworks (1854-56), Irton Waterworks and Oliver's Mount reservoir (1881).

Edward Filliter served his pupillage as a civil engineer at the East London waterworks and thereafter specialised in such work.

In Scarborough he was resident engineer for extensions to the waterworks between 1854 and 1856. Although he settled in Leeds about 1856, where he became Borough surveyor and later a consulting civil engineer, he continued to advise the Scarborough Waterworks Company. In 1871 he drew up plans for a new pumping station at Cayton, and when Scarborough Council bought the waterworks at Cayton Bay and Osgodby in 1878 he produced a detailed report on the Borough's water supply and a further report in 1879. Edward Filliter recommended the construction of new waterworks at Irton which were built to his design in 1881. He superintended all the work which included the mains and a reservoir on Oliver's Mount.

References – (9), (14), (61), (85j).

FOWLER, Charles Hodgson   **Durham architect**
1840 (Southwell) - 1910 (The College, Durham)

Scarborough work - St John the Evangelist Church, St Sepulchre St
(1884), restoration of St Martin's Seamer (1887-8), restoration of St
Thomas's Church East Sandgate (1889), St Mary's Parish Church - screen,
pulpit & lectern (1897).

Charles Fowler, the son of a parson, was a pupil of the architect Sir George
Gilbert Scott (1811-1878). Fowler became an Associate of the Royal
Institute of British Architects in 1863 and a Fellow in 1870 and set up in
practice in Durham. Between 1874 and 1876 he was involved in the
restoration of Durham Cathedral with Scott. Fowler specialised in the
restoration and maintenance of church buildings and at various times was
architect to the cathedrals at Durham, Lincoln, Rochester and York. In
Yorkshire he restored numerous churches, many in the East Riding being
commissioned by Sir Tatton Sykes of Sledmere.
In Scarborough Charles Fowler designed St John the Evangelist Mission
Church in St Sepulchre Street (opened October 1884) and restored St
Thomas's Church, East Sandgate in 1889. For the parish Church of St
Mary he designed a screen, pulpit and lectern and at nearby Seamer he
restored St Martin's Parish Church.
Charles Hodgson Fowler died in Durham on the 14th of December 1910.
References - (14), (18), (21), (23), (25), (32), (33), (44), (46), (54), (57),
(85j), (92a), (92b), (92c), (94), (101), (102), (113).

GIBSON, John   **Malton architect, builder & surveyor**
1811 (Brompton) - 1887 (Malton)

Scarborough work - Crown Hotel and Esplanade terrace, Esplanade Hotel
and Belmont Terrace (1841-6).

John Gibson was apprenticed as a carpenter and joiner to a firm of
Scarborough builders and about 1841 he started his own business. He was
consulted by the South Cliff Company on the best way to lay out and
develop land they had bought from Scarborough Corporation. The
company had previously consulted the York architect Richard Sharp (q.v.)
and the Hull surveyor David Thorpe but found both opinions
unsatisfactory. Dr Thomas Weddell, a member of South Cliff Company,
then approached Gibson who was his patient at the time. The directors
accepted Gibson's plans and on the 8th October 1842 the first brick of
Esplanade Terrace was laid. It was completed in 1845 with the Crown
Hotel as its centrepiece. Gibson was also responsible for Belmont Terrace

(now the Esplanade Hotel) and the roads linking the overall development to the Cliff Bridge and to the Spa.

In 1846 John Gibson moved his business to Malton where he became the leading architect and the main builder and surveyor of mid-Victorian Malton and Norton. His son John (1849-82) entered the business which became "John Gibson & Son" and in 1882 Gibson took his assistant C.H. Channon into partnership, as "John Gibson, Son & Channon".

John Gibson died in Malton in 1887 at the age of 76.

References - (2), (14), (21), (36a), (44), (49), (84), (85j), (85k), (85), (92a), (92c), (103).

GOLDIE, George   **Sheffield & London architect**
1828 (York) - 1887 (Brittany)

Scarborough work - St Peter's Roman Catholic Church, Castle Rd, 1858 (completed 1874).

George Goldie was a pupil of the Sheffield architects' firm "Weightman and Hadfield" (John Gray Weightman 1801-1872 and Matthew Ellison Hadfield 1812-1885) and later a partner as "Weightman, Hadfield & Goldie". Goldie, who became an Associate of the Royal Institute of British Architects in 1853, was of a Roman Catholic family, two of his brothers becoming catholic priests and another brother, Charles an artist, while George specialised in designing Roman Catholic Churches.

In Scarborough the firm of "Weightman, Hadfield and Goldie" of Sheffield and London was chosen to design a new Roman Catholic Church to replace the 1809 chapel in Auborough Street. George Goldie actually produced the design which he exhibited at the Royal Academy in London in 1859. Although opened in July 1858, the church was incomplete due to lack of funds and the presbytery was not added until 1861 and it was 1874 before Goldie's design was finally completed. Goldie designed much of the interior decoration and his brother Charles did the paintings in the apse above the reredos. Canon Walker, the founder of St Peter's, died in 1873 and George Goldie designed the memorial to him.

George Goldie was a prolific architect of Roman Catholic churches throughout England, Scotland and Ireland. Examples in Yorkshire include St Anne's, Ugthorpe (1855-57), St Wilfrid's, Duncome Place, York (1862-64), St Joseph's, Richmond (1867-68), and the Sacred Heart Church, Northallerton, (1870).

George Goldie died at St Sevran, Brittany on the 1st of March 1887 and is buried at St Jouan des Guerets.

References - (14), (18), (21), (44), (46), (50), (54), (57), (73), (81), (85j), (92a), (92b), (92c), (101).

HALL, John   **Scarborough architect**
1851 (York) - 1914 (Scarborough)

Scarborough work - Albert Hall, Aberdeen Walk (1878, collapsed 1942), Salvation Army Barracks, Alma Parade (1881), offices for "Scarborough Mercury", Aberdeen Terrace (1882), conversion of baths to School of Art, Vernon Place (1884, destroyed 1941), Lawn Tennis Club pavilion, West St (1885).
see also "Hall, Cooper & Davis" and "Hall & Tugwell"

John Hall came to Scarborough sometime before 1874 and established his architect's office at 102, Westborough.   Besides having a domestic practice, designing houses and villas, Hall was also responsible for several public buildings. These included the Albert Hall, in Aberdeen Walk for Mr John Dawber (1878), a building with cellarage, two shops and a large hall for use of the Scarborough Liberal Club. Hall also designed the Salvation Army 'barracks' in Alma Parade for General Booth (1881) and offices for the "Scarborough Mercury" in Aberdeen Terrace (1882). New Public Baths at the corner of Vernon Place and Falconer Road had been designed by C.A.Bury (q.v.) and opened in 1883. However, in 1884 John Hall was responsible for converting them to the use of Scarborough School of Art involving, amongst other things, the addition of a new exhibition hall. In the same year he submitted plans in a competition for a Methodist Church on South Cliff coming second to "Morley and Woodhouse" (q.v.).
From 1886 to 1894 John Hall was in partnership with his ex-pupil Frank Tugwell (q.v.) as "Hall & Tugwell" (q.v.). One of the pupils of "Hall & Tugwell" was Thomas Edwin Cooper (q.v.) who later John Hall took into partnership with Herbert Davis (q.v.) as "Hall, Cooper & Davis" (q.v.).
After 1903, when both Cooper and Davis had left the partnership, John Hall continued in practice, later taking his son, John Percy Hall (q.v.) as a partner, the firm becoming "John Hall and Son".
John Hall was killed at his home in Westbourne Park in the German bombardment of Scarborough on the 16th December 1914.
References – (14), (36a), (57), (77), (85j), (90), (94).

HALL, John Percy   **Scarborough architect**
1876 (Barrow in Furness) - 1939

Scarborough work – none known.
see John Hall & Son

John Percy Hall was the son of the Scarborough architect John Hall (q.v.) He studied at Scarborough School of Art and was articled to his father. He set up in practice in 1903 in London and also in Scarborough where he was in partnership with his father until 1914 as "John Hall & Son" (q.v.). By 1913 J.P.Hall was an Associate of the Royal Institute of British Architects, and after his father's death in 1914, Hall worked only from his Kensington office. He specialised in large country houses and industrial buildings. He was also responsible for alterations to a house in Bournemouth for Sir Joseph Compton Ricket PC MP for whom "Hall, Cooper & Davis" (q.v.) had designed "Seacroft Mansions" in Scarborough in 1901.

References - (14), (36a), (100), (101), (122), (123), (124).

HALL, John & Son   **Scarborough architects' firm**
John Hall (1851-1914)
John Percy Hall (1876-1939)
fl. 1905-1914

Scarborough work – additions to skating rink (1901), drill hall, St John's Rd (1910), new wing for "Southlands", West St (1913).

John Hall (q.v.) was in partnership with his son John Percy Hall (q.v.) from about 1905 to 1914 when John Hall was killed.
As well as domestic work the firm designed additions to the skating rink of Foreshore Road for the "Grand Skating Rink Co." (1910), a drill hall in St John's Road for the Territorial Association (1910) and a new wing to the "Southlands" Hotel on West Street for the "South Cliff Boarding House Co." (1913).

References – (36a), (94).

HALL, COOPER & DAVIS   **Scarborough architects' firm**
John Hall (1851-1914)
Thomas Edwin Cooper (1874 - 1942)
Herbert Davis (1872 -)
fl. 1896-1903

Scarborough work – extensions to Falsgrave Methodist Chapel, Seamer Rd (1897), Scarborough College, Filey Rd (1898), Warwick's Revolving Tower (1898 demolished 1906), Gas Company cottages, Seamer Rd (1899), Higher Grade School, Westwood (1900), "Seacroft Mansions", Filey Rd (1901).

About 1896 John Hall (q.v.) took into partnership his ex-pupil Thomas Edwin Cooper (q.v.) and Herbert Davis (q.v.) to form the firm of "Hall, Cooper & Davis" with offices at 24, Westborough, Scarborough and also in

London. The partnership lasted until about 1903.

"Hall, Cooper & Davis" had a considerable domestic practice in Scarborough and besides designing houses, they also worked for public undertakings. For "Scarborough Gas Co." they designed 13 cottages on Seamer Road (1899). For the "Scarborough Electric Supply Company" they designed 2 cottages in Salisbury Road (1899) and a boiler house, Seamer Road and an engine house, Salisbury Street (1900). For the Scarborough School Board their design for a Higher Grade School was built at Westwood having been chosen by competition. For the "Wesleyan College Co." they designed a new college on Filey Road (1898). They were the architects for the non-engineering aspects of Warwick's Tower (1897) (see Thomas Warwick) and in the same year won a competition for extensions to Falsgrave Wesleyan Methodist Chapel, on Seamer Road. In 1901 the firm designed the house "Seacroft Mansions" for Sir Joseph Compton Ricket.

The firm exhibited several of these designs at the Royal Academy including "School, Scarborough" (1898), "New College, Scarborough", "Houses at Scalby" and "Gas Company, Scarborough" (all 1899).

References - (19), (36a), (54), (92a), (94).

HALL & TUGWELL   **Scarborough architects' firm**
John Hall (1851-1914)
Frank Tugwell (1862-1940)
fl. 1886-1894

Scarborough work - Fish Salesmen's Offices, West Pier (1886), Ramshill Hotel alterations (1886), rebuilding of the Equestrian Hotel, St Thomas Street (1886), "Holbeck Hirst", Esplanade (1889), London Yorkshire Bank, corner Huntriss Row & Westborough now NatWest PLC (1890), Gladstone Rd Schools (1890), rebuilding of Bull Hotel, Westborough (1890), new Coastguard House, South Foreshore (1890), Hospital and Dispensary, Friars Entry (1893 demolished 1976), Pavilion, Scarborough Cricket Club (1894), Liberal Club, Westborough (1894), "Normanton Rise", Holbeck Hill (1894).

John Hall (q.v.) took his ex-pupil Frank Tugwell (q.v.) into partnership to form "Hall & Tugwell" which existed from about 1886 to 1894 when Tugwell left to set up his own practice. One of the pupils of "Hall & Tugwell" was Thomas Edwin Cooper (q.v.).

In Scarborough "Hall & Tugwell" were responsible for several villas including "Normanton Rise", West Street for Major John Greaves Smirthwaite and "Holbeck Hurst", Esplanade for Robert Marillier (q.v.). After Marillier's death in 1903 Alfred Shuttleworth (1843-1925) bought

37

and demolished the house to improve his view from "Red Court" designed by "Bedford & Kitson" (q.v.) and created the "Shuttleworth Gardens" on the site. "Hall & Tugwell" also prepared plans for the rebuilding of several public houses. Their main public works were the London & Yorkshire Bank (corner of Huntriss Row and Newborough 1890), Scarborough Hospital and Dispensary (1891), and the Liberal Club, Westborough (now the "Lord Rosebery") (1894). The firm also designed Gladstone Road Schools (1890) which were opened by the Right Honourable Anthony John Mundella MP (1825-97). The Scarborough Gazette commented of the schools that "passers-by would not commend the exterior for any beauty of appearance whatever" but at least the interior layout was praised.
References - (36a), (46), (85j), (92a), (94), (118).

HANSTOCK Walter   **Batley architect**
1843 (Chesterfield) - 1900

Scarborough work - carriage works, Swan Hill Rd (1889).

Walter Hanstock, an Associate of the Royal Institute of British Architects, designed some carriage works in Swan Hill Road for his father-in-law John Blackburn - a woollen merchant of "Rose Bank", Valley Road, Scarborough .
References – (14), (44), (94), (101).

HARE, Henry Thomas   **London architect**
1861 (Scarborough) - 1921 (Farnham)

Scarborough work – domestic.

Henry Thomas Hare, the son of the Scarborough photographer and fine art dealer Haydon Hare, was articled to the local architect C.A.Bury (q.v.) from 1876 to 1880.
In Scarborough he prepared plans for new villas in Falsgrave for Captain William Baxter - a ship owner and for a house and shop in St Thomas Street for William Sleightholm (1881) but soon after he left to further his career.
After spending a year in Paris at the École des Beaux Arts he worked with the London architects Zephaniah King (1834-1906) and Richard Harris Hill (fl.1855-1910). Between 1885 and 1886 Henry Hare travelled around England, France and Belgium studying architecture and sketching. In 1886 he was awarded the Ashpitel prize for the most distinguished candidate in the Royal Institute of British Architects examinations and became an Associate in 1887 and a Fellow 3 years later. He set up in independent

practice in London in 1891 and was associated for a time with another of C. A.Bury's ex-pupils Thomas Davison (q.v.)

Hare became known for his designs of municipal buildings many of which were won in open competition such as Oxford Town Hall and Staffordshire County Council Buildings, Stafford (both 1892). He is particularly associated with library design such as those at Harrogate (1906) and Wolverhampton (1902). He also exhibited extensively at the Royal Academy in London from 1890 to 1920.

He retired about 1911 but during the First World War he was sent to France to advise on the preservation of French Chateaux where British troops were billeted, and from 1917 to 1919 Henry Hare was President of the Royal Institute of British Architects. After the War he became involved with post-war housing schemes and he directed the Great Housing Competition of 1919.

Henry Hare died at Farnham Common in January 1921.

References - (14), (18), (34), (41), (44), (50), (54), (55), (57), (85j), (85k), (92b), (92c), (92f), (92g), (92j), (92k), (94), (100), (101), (122).

HAWES, John Cyril   **London architect**
1877 (Richmond) -

Scarborough work - St Saviour's (temporary) Church, Gladstone Rd (1898).

John C.Hawes of New Cross, London had produced a registered design for an "iron church", essentially a temporary structure to be erected to solve an urgent need for a church. This design was chosen for the first St Saviour's Church in Gladstone Road and erected in 1898. The church, which held 350 people, was used as a church hall once the present church of St Saviour was built in 1902 to the design of J.T. Micklethwaite (q.v.).

References - (14), (54), (85j), (85k).

HELYER, Henry Thomas   **architect & surveyor**

fl. Sc 1867

Scarborough work – none known.

Henry Thomas Helyer was listed in the Scarborough directory for 1867 as an architect and surveyor of Westborough, living at 3, Montpellier Terrace. This may be the Isle of Wight architect (Henry) Thomas Helyer (1811-1894) who designed St James's Church at Seacroft Leeds (1845-6) and who exhibited at the Royal Academy between 1846 and 1862.

References – (14), (36a), (54), (92b).

HILDYARD Elias   **assistant borough surveyor**
1857 (Scarborough) - post 1887

Scarborough work – new kitchens, Shakespeare Hotel, St Helen's Square (1885), alterations to the Victoria Hotel, Westborough (1886).

In 1881 Elias Hildyard was assistant to the Scarborough Borough Surveyor Joseph Petch (q.v.).
However, between 1884 and 1887 Hildyard prepared plans for a variety of private projects including new houses and alterations and additions to several hotels including the Shakespeare Hotel for the brewer Eden Heywood Gawne, and the Victoria Hotel for John Thomas Melton.
References – (14), (94).

HOLT, Henry Percy   **Leeds civil engineer**
1848 (Wakefield) - 1903 (London)

Scarborough work - Queen's Parade Tramway (1878, demolished 1888).

Henry Percy Holt was a pupil of his father, also Henry, a civil engineer of Leeds and Wakefield, under whom he gained experience in railways, drainage and waterworks. He then worked throughout the country and in Europe at the main railway centres. In 1872 he commenced business as a consulting civil engineer in Leeds and was in charge of many industrial projects. He was elected an Associate of the Institution of Civil Engineers in 1875 and a Member in 1898.
In Scarborough he designed the Queen's Parade Tramway (1878) - a cliff tramway which ran from Queen's Parade to the shore near the Promenade Pier built by Eugenius Birch (q.v.). Like the South Cliff Tramway, to which he was consulting engineer, it also worked on a water counterbalance system. However, within 10 years the Queen's Parade Tramway was unsafe. Scarborough Council bought it from the Queen's Parade Tramway Company and demolished it as part of their general improvements to the North Cliff. Also while working in Scarborough, Holt tried unsuccessfully to generate interest in building an incline tramway on Oliver's Mount.
References – (14), (64), (85j).

Primitive Methodist Jubilee Chapel. Aberdeen Walk (1861-1966) by W. Baldwin Stewart (see pg 75)

41

Constitutional (Conservative) Club, Huntriss Row (1888) by H.A Cheers (see page 20)

42

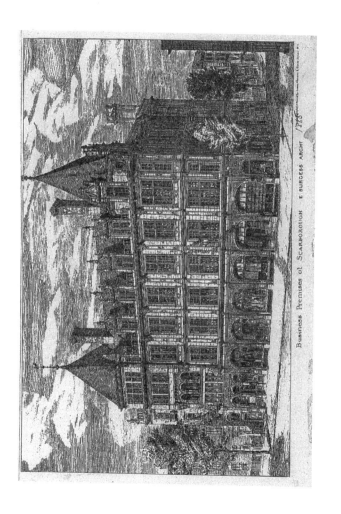

Business Premises at SCARBOROUGH   E BURGESS ARCHT

William Rowntree's Department Store. 33-39. Westborough (1882-1990) by Edward Burgess (see pg 17)

The Building News, Mar. 7, 1884.

New Church of S. John Scarborough. C. Hodgson Fowler, F.S.A. Architect.

St John's Mission Church. St Sepulchre Street (1884) by C.H.Fowler (see pg.33)

HOWKINS John   **Edinburgh harbour engineer**
1839 (Granton) - 1906 (Granton)

Scarborough work - Scarborough Harbour improvements (1878-1881)

John Howkins, the son of a Scottish engineer, became a pupil with the engineer James Leslie (q.v.) who specialised in harbour works. Howkins worked throughout the country gaining experience on harbour, dock and railway projects. He became an Associate of the Institution of Civil Engineers in 1867 and a Member in 1872.

John Howkins set up in private practice in Edinburgh in 1868 but in 1870 moved to Hartlepool as engineer to the Port and Harbour Commissioners. He returned to Granton in 1877 to take up his father's position as engineer and general superintendent of Granton Harbour but remained consulting engineer to Hartlepool.

In Scarborough John Howkins was consulted in 1878 by the Scarborough Harbour Commissioners to survey the harbour. His recommendations included plans for general improvements such as deepening both harbours, widening and extending the west pier, removing the island pier and under-building the old quay walls. Howkin's plans were accepted by the both Scarborough Corporation and by the Harbour Commissioners and the work, for which Robert Wyld (q.v.) was resident engineer, was completed early in 1881.

John Howkins died in Granton in 1906

References – (61), (64), (85j), (99).

HUNT, Richard   **patentee & hotel keeper**
1813 (York) - post 1876
fl.Sc 1867-1876

Scarborough work - South Cliff Tramway (1876).

Richard Hunt was proprietor of the Prince of Wales Hotel, Esplanade, Scarborough from at least 1861 until his death about 1878. In 1867 Councillor Hunt argued the case for an incline railway joining Esplanade to the Spa promenade and had "Shelford & Robinson" of Westminster draw up plans. However, neither the Cliff Bridge Company, through whose land the railway would pass, nor Scarborough Corporation supported the plan. In 1870 an unsuccessful request was put to the Corporation by Peter Penn Gaskell to build a tramway from the sands to South Cliff near Belmont Road and in the following year the residents of South Cliff petitioned for such a railway. In 1872 Richard Hunt submitted plans which were approved. The next year a prospectus for the South Cliff Tramway

Company was issued with Richard Hunt as chief promoter, William Harrington Lucas (q.v.) as engineer and "Stewart & Bury" (q.v.) as architects. The company offices were at the Prince of Wales Hotel.

In 1875 Richard Hunt filed a patent (1875 no. 3926) for an invention entitled "Carriages and Traction Apparatus for Steep Inclines" which was granted the following year. The invention was for a gravitational system of propulsion for an incline railway whereby sea water was pumped into and released from tanks to raise and lower the carriages. Although such a system had been used for many years in industrial settings this was its first use for passenger carriage. The South Cliff Tramway was built opposite Hunt's Hotel and was operating by 1876. Hunt died sometime before August 1878 when some Canadians came to Scarborough specially to inspect his invention.

The tramway was closed for a short time in 1878 for alterations and was re-opened after a safety inspection by H.P.Holt of Leeds (q.v.). Further work was done in 1879 when a report in the Scarborough Gazette said that although people had jeered at Mr Hunt's original idea, the tramway was now such a success that a new steam engine to operate the pumps had been installed. The chimney for the engine was at a house on South Cliff but, as newspaper reported, "if you don't know where it is you will not spot it". With the re-opening for the 1878 season, dogs were now allowed to travel for one penny but "dirty or wet dogs" were prohibited.

It is not known if Hunt was an engineer or whether he personally drew up the meticulous drawings included in his patent application, which was witnessed by Bristow Hunt, a London solicitor and patent agent, and possibly a relative.

References – (16), (36a), (85j), (94), (95), (118).

IRVIN, John   **architect & borough surveyor**
1825 - 1853

Scarborough work - Market Hall, St Helen's Square (1853).

John Irvin was Scarborough's Borough Surveyor and surveyor to the Improvement Commissioners when, in 1851, he was asked to prepare plans for a new enclosed public market in the town. He visited several newly-built market halls in other towns and his plans were completed by June 1851. He chose a site and clearance work began in 1852. Parliamentary approval for the new market hall came with the Scarborough Public Market Act (1852) and building began the main contractor being John Shaftoe of York.

John Irvin died in May 1853 and so did not see the opening of his Market Hall in August of that year.

G.T.Andrews (q.v.) was appointed architect to the Market Company after Irvin's death.

References - (22), (46), (85j), (92a), (104), (106), (111).

IVESON James Albert   **Scarborough architect**
fl.Sc 1893 - 1931

Scarborough works - Phthisis Hospital, Dean Rd Workhouse (1911).

James Iveson is listed in the 1893 directory as an architect and surveyor at the Estate Office at Hackness Hall near Scarborough (Lord Derwent's Estate). However, by 1897 he had moved into Scarborough where, from 1903 onwards, he worked for the Board of Guardians. He prepared plans for a variety of additions and alterations to the Dean Road Workhouse including a new Phthisis (Tuberculosis) Hospital. In the early 1930s Iveson was at nearby Newby.

References - (36a), (94).

KELLY, John   **Leeds & London architect**
1840 (Dewsbury) - 1904

Scarborough work - none known.

John Kelly came to Scarborough with his family at the age of about six. He was articled to the Scarborough architect John Petch (1819-97) (q.v.) and later went to Manchester where he worked for John Medland Taylor (1834-1909). He then worked in London for three years with George Edmund Street (1824-81) where another pupil was J.D.Sedding (q.v.). Kelly set up in partnership with Richard Adams (1841-83) in Leeds in about 1866.
John Kelly was architect to the Leeds School Board for 20 years but then returned to practise in London. He designed numerous schools, flats, houses, hotels and more than 50 churches.

References – (14), (18), (44), (54), (73), (94).

KITSON, Sydney Decimus   **Leeds architect**
1871 (Leeds) - 1937

Scarborough work – alterations to bank, 28, Huntriss Row, now Sydenham's shop (1904).
see also "Bedford & Kitson"

Sydney Kitson was articled to the architect E J May (q.v.) and from 1897 to 1903 was in partnership with Francis Bedford. In 1904 Sydney Kitson drew up plans for alterations to the premises of the London City and Midland Bank at 28, Huntriss Row, Scarborough.

References- (14), (18), (44), (94), (122), (123), (124).

KNOWLES, George   architect & civil engineer
1776 - 1856 (Scarborough)

Scarborough work - Spa gardens, drainage etc. (1837-40).

George Knowles was a contractor, civil engineer and architect working in Ireland in the first two decades of the 19th century. He was architect and contractor for the Royal Canal in Dublin, producing designs for Mullingar Harbour and the Sheriff Street Bridge over the Canal (1808). He designed and built the Lucan Bridge (1814). He was contractor for the Richmond (now O'Donovan Rossa) Bridge (1812-16) and designed and built Whitworth (now Father Matthew) Bridge (1816-17) both over the River Liffey in Dublin.

From about 1821 to 1825 he was living at "Lucan House", Sharow, (near Ripon) North Yorkshire where he designed and superintended the building of the Church of St John (1825).

Knowles moved to Scarborough about 1836 where he resided at "Wood End" (now the Natural History Museum). From about 1837 to about 1851 Knowles was a committee member of the Scarborough Cliff Bridge Company which managed the Scarborough Spa. He was responsible for preparing plans and designs for laying out the Spa Gardens and draining the South Cliff in the vicinity. In 1844 George Knowles published a pamphlet vehemently opposing the proposed York to Scarborough railway line. He claimed that it would fill the town with " ... vagrants and those who have no money to spend ... ". The managers of the Spa, however, could see the opportunities offered by the railway, which was opened the following year.

George Knowles died at "Wood End", Scarborough on the 23rd June 1856 and was buried at Sharow in the church that he had designed, where there is a memorial to him by Thomas Milnes.

It is not known who designed and built "Wood End", but probably it was erected in the mid-1830s. Given Knowles' background and the fact that he took up residence at "Wood End" about 1836 there must be a possibility that the house is of his own design.

References - (14), (26), (28), (36a), (42), (66), (72), (79), (85j), (85m), (87), (92b), (101), (118).

LESLIE, James   **Scottish civil engineer**
1801 (Largo, Fife) - 1889

Scarborough work - Spa sea wall and promenade (1830s), Spa cliff stabilisation work (1840s), South Sands sewage drainage system, (1853).

James Leslie was an eminent civil engineer specialising in harbours, docks, sea defences, reservoirs and embankments whose advice was sought throughout the world.
The Scarborough Cliff Bridge Company, which owned and managed the Spa, frequently consulted "the Scottish engineer Mr Leslie", during the late 1830s and the 1840s. It is probable that this was James Leslie who had worked under the direction of William Chapman (q.v.) from 1828 at Leith during the construction of new docks and a breakwater.
For the Scarborough Cliff Bridge Company Leslie appears to have been responsible for the design and construction of the Spa sea wall at the time that Henry Wyatt (q.v.) was supervising the erection of his "Gothic Saloon" which opened in 1839. Also at the Spa, later in the 1840s, Leslie advised on remedial work for the continuing cliff slippage.
For the Scarborough Improvement Commissioners Leslie prepared plans for a means of conveying sewage over the south sands which were considered and agreed to in 1853.
James Leslie died on the 29th December 1889.

References – (14), (64), (85j), (118).

LOCKWOOD & MAWSON   **Bradford architects' firm**
Henry Francis Lockwood (1811 Doncaster -1878 Richmond, London)
William Mawson (1828 Leeds -1889 Bradford)
Richard Mawson (1834 Leeds -1904)
fl. 1849-1874

Scarborough work - Congregational Church, Ramshill Rd (1865), Baptist Church, Albemarle Crescent (1867).

"Lockwood & Mawson" designed many of the public buildings in Bradford. They were architects to the nearby Saltaire Estate, built for Sir Titus Salt (1803-1876), which included a Congregational Church (1858-9), alpaca mills, workers' houses etc.
In Scarborough, in 1863, it was proposed to build a new Congregational Church because the Bar Church was overcrowded with visitors in summer and services had to be held in the Mechanics' Hall. Titus Salt was a leading promoter of the new church and he and his architect Henry

Lockwood visited Scarborough to view a site on Ramshill Road, considered one of the best in the town. Lockwood submitted plans in 1864 for a gothic-style church capable of holding 1,000 - 1,200 people, with an estimated cost £9,000. The Scarborough Gazette reported that "as visitors to the town have a special interest in this church the committee is largely composed of gentlemen from a distance". Salt gave the site for the church while donations for the building fund came from as far as Sheffield, Leeds, Manchester, Saltaire, York, Huddersfield, Ashton-under-Lyne, Bradford and Stockport as well as Scarborough. The Church was opened in 1865.

In 1866 a breakaway group of Scarborough Baptists, which had been holding services in the Mechanics' Hall, bought a site in Albemarle Crescent and appointed "Lockwood & Mawson" to design a new church. Albemarle Baptist Church was opened in 1867.

The Scarborough building contractor for both the Congregational Church and the Baptist Church was John Barry (1833-1910 q.v.). In 1868 he was awarded the contract to build a new Workhouse for the Haslingden (Lancashire) Board of Guardians, the architects for which were "Lockwood & Mawson".

References - (14), (18), (44), (46), (54), (73), (75), (85a), (85c), (85j), (92a), (92b), (92c).

LORIMER (Sir) Robert Stodart   Edinburgh architect
1864 (Edinburgh) - 1929 (Edinburgh)

Scarborough work – house, Weaponness Park (1900)

Robert Lorimer was, for a short period in 1889, draughtsman to "Bodley & Garner" (G.F.Bodley q.v. and Thomas Garner 1839-1906). Lorimer became an Associate of the Royal Institute of British Architects in 1890 and a Fellow in 1906. In 1893 he set up in independent practice in Edinburgh and became a major Scottish architect of his time. He created a Scottish form of the "arts and crafts" tradition and also built or totally re-modelled about 50 country houses in Britain. He designed the Thistle Chapel in St Giles Cathedral and the Scottish National War Memorial in Edinburgh Castle. He was architect to Imperial War Graves Commission.

In Scarborough, in 1900, before becoming so well known, Lorimer was invited by Sir Arthur Herbert Dyke Acland (1847-1926) to design a house for him in Weaponness Park and to add a summer house in the following year. Acland, who had recently come to live in Scarborough after being Liberal MP for Rotherham from 1885-99, was an educational reformer, remembered for increasing the school leaving age to eleven and ending "payment by results" in English education.

References - (14), (44), (54), (76), (94), (101), (122), (123), (124).

LUCAS, William Harrington　　　　　　　　　civil engineer
1837 (Surrey) –
fl.Sc 1873

Scarborough work - (engineer to) South Cliff Tramway, Esplanade
(1876).

W.H.Lucas trained as a mechanical engineer and became an Associate of
the Institution of Civil Engineers in 1866. He was the engineer responsible
for the South Cliff Tramway which opened in 1876. The main promotor of
the project was Richard Hunt (q.v.), opposite whose "Prince of Wales
Hotel" the tramway was built, the architects being "Stewart & Bury" (q.v.).

References – (14), (61), (85j), (95).

McADAM, John Loudon　　　　　　　　Scottish road engineer
1756 (Ayr) - 1836

Scarborough work - York-Scarborough Road improvements (1822).

John McAdam made a fortune in his uncle's counting house in New York
and returned to Scotland in 1783 buying an estate in Ayrshire. Here he
began experimenting with a revolutionary method of road construction. In
1816 he was appointed surveyor to Bristol Turnpike Trust remaking roads
with crushed stone bound with gravel and raised to improve drainage which
became known as the "Macadamised System". His advice was widely
sought and in 1827 he was appointed "Surveyor General of Metropolitan
Roads".
In 1821 the Yorkshire Gazette carried a long article about the poor state of
the road from York to Scarborough. The parishes along its route, which
were responsible for its upkeep, were being threatened with indictment by
the General Post Office and they asked McAdam to make
recommendations. He visited Scarborough and wrote a long report. "Mr
McAdam & Son" were then appointed surveyors for the York to
Scarborough Road to put the road into a "competent state of affairs to hold
out inducements to travellers more frequently to visit Scarborough". The
next year, 1822, the Yorkshire Gazette reported that the road had been
much improved by Mr McAdam. As a result several new developments
had occurred in Scarborough including a new range of houses built by Mr
Southwell, a "complete and elegant change to the baths on the cliff", and
now a new steam packet from London to Leith called at the Harbour.
References - (76), (85m), (108).

MARILLIER, Robert Aspland　　　　　　　　　　　civil engineer
1826 (Harrow) - 1903 (Torquay)

Scarborough works - none.

While not strictly a "Scarborough engineer" Robert Marillier deserves a mention as an engineer who retired to Scarborough and became Mayor of the Borough.

Robert Marillier was articled to a noted London water engineer Thomas Wicksteed. After completing his apprenticeship Marillier took charge of Hull waterworks in 1845, an appointment he held until 1861. From 1861 to 1865 he was engineer to Hull Local Board of Health and then was appointed engineer to the Hull Dock Company, a post he held until 1893 when the Company taken over by North Eastern Railway Co. Marillier personally superintended the construction of the Sir William Wright Dock, St Andrew's Dock (the fish dock) and two large graving (dry) docks, all in Hull.

Robert Marillier came to live in Scarborough in 1884 and commuted to Hull until he retired in 1893. In 1890 he had a large house built at the far south end of Esplanade designed by "Hall & Tugwell" (q.v.) and called "Holbeck Hurst".

Marillier became a Scarborough councillor in 1895 and was elected Mayor in 1896. He died on the 13th of February 1903 in Torquay.

"Holbeck Hurst" was bought and demolished by the Lincoln engineer Alfred Shuttleworth (1843-1925) in order to improve the view from his house "Red Court" designed by "Bedford & Kitson" (q.v.), the site now being the "Shuttleworth Gardens".

References - (9), (14), (36a), (94).

MAY, Edward John　　　　　　　　　　　　　**London architect**
1853 (Clapham) - 1941

Scarborough work – "May Lodge", Filey Rd (1885).

Edward May was articled to the architect Decimus Burton (1800-80) being his last pupil. May worked in many architects' offices including that of Richard Norman Shaw (1831-1912) about 1876 and became an Associate of the Royal Institute of British Architects in 1881 and a Fellow in 1887.

In 1885 a Scarborough surgeon and general practitioner, Dr Charles Hutchinson, asked E.J.May to design a house for him which was built as "May Lodge" on Filey Road. May was a frequent exhibitor at the Royal Academy in London and in 1886 he exhibited a design entitled 'House at Scarborough' presumably Dr Hutchinson's house.

Although a Roman Catholic May was appointed architect to the "Church of England Waifs and Strays Society" and in this capacity designed some additions and alterations to 6, Belgrave Crescent, Scarborough in 1906.
References - (14), (36a), (44), (54), (94), (101) (122), (123), (124).

MESSENT, Philip John   civil engineer
1831 (London) -post 1896

Scarborough work – consultant engineer to Scarborough Council 1887 & 1896.

Philip Messent had been involved with the construction of Yarmouth Bridge and later was resident engineer for the Tyne Piers works. Scarborough Council had engaged one of Messent's former pupils, Robert Aytoun (q.v.), in 1887 as resident engineer for the construction of Royal Albert Drive and consulted him on the state of the old pier at Scarborough Harbour. Aytoun's proposals were estimated at £6,000 leading the Council to seek a second opinion from Philip Messent. In the main it was Messent's report that was used to carry out the work.
Messent was consulted again by Scarborough Council at the commencement of the construction of Marine Drive in 1896.
References - (14), (62), (85j), (85k), (114).

MICKLETHWAITE, John Thomas   London architect
1843 - 1906 (London)

Scarborough work - St Saviour's Church, Gladstone Rd (1902).

John Micklethwaite was a pupil of Sir George Gilbert Scott (1811-78) after which he went into independent practice in 1869. From 1876 to 1892 he was in partnership with Somers Clark (1841-1926) another of Scott's pupils. J.T.Micklethwaite was a church architect and wrote the book "Modern Parish Churches". In 1898 he was appointed surveyor to the Dean and Chapter of Westminster Abbey and in 1900 architect to St George's Chapel, Windsor.
In Scarborough J.T.Micklethwaite designed St Saviour's Church, Gladstone Road the building of which was supervised by Charles Edeson (q.v.) and opened in 1902. It replaced the previous "iron church" built in 1898 to a registered design by J.C.Hawes (q.v.).
References - (18), (25), (44), (46), (54), (57), (85j), (85k), (92a), (92b), (99), (101).

MIDDLEMISS, George Andrew   **Sunderland architect**
1815 (Co. Durham) - post 1860

Scarborough work - alterations and improvements to Theatre Royal, St Thomas St (1857-60).

George Middlemiss advertised in the Scarborough Mercury in 1857 for tenders for alterations to the Theatre Royal in St Thomas Street, Scarborough. The plans could be seen at Mr Crosby's office in Scarborough or at the architect's office in Fawcett Street, Sunderland. Middlemiss stated that he would visit the theatre to explain the details of his improvements. When the Theatre Royal re-opened in June 1860 the Scarborough Gazette reported that the external and internal alterations had been so extensive that it was, in effect, an entirely new building. Middlemiss had supervised all of the works. The artist and scene painter, William Roxby Beverely (1811-1889), designed the decoration of the Theatre.
Scarborough's Theatre Royal was, at this time, owned and managed by the Roxby family who also had theatres at Shields, Sunderland and Durham hence the use of a Sunderland architect.
References - (7), (14), (44), (85j), (85k).

MILLHOUSE, William   **Scarborough civil engineer**
1848 (Scarborough) - post 1914

Scarborough work - (engineer to) Scarborough waterworks from 1880.

William Millhouse was articled to "Martin & Fenwick", civil engineers of Leeds, from 1865-70 and worked with them until 1879.
Millhouse moved to Scarborough to become an assistant in the office of the Borough Surveyor, Joseph Petch (1821-97 q.v.). In 1880 Millhouse was appointed resident engineer and manager of the Corporation Waterworks which at that time were being extended under the direction of the consulting engineer Edward Filliter (q.v.).
Millhouse continued as the water engineer into the 20th century and in 1908 published an article about the waterworks in the Journal of the British Association of Water-Works Engineers.
References - (14), (36a), (61), (85j), (94).

MORGAN Thomas F   **Hull engineer**
1846 (Sleights) - post 1881

Scarborough work - (engineer to) Central Tramway (1881).

Thomas Morgan was appointed engineer to The Central Tramway Company to build an incline railway from Marine Promenade (St Nicholas Cliff) to Scarborough Sands in 1881. Charles Bury (q.v.) was architect for the project. The upper station was built on the site of the photographic studio of John Inskip (1833-1909), but a new studio was built for him on the first floor of the new station.

References – (8), (14), (85j), (94).

MORLEY, William James   **Bradford architect**
1847 (Garforth) - 1930 (Heaton W Yorks)

Scarborough work - South Cliff Methodist Church (1886).

William Morley was articled to the Leeds architects "Lockwood & Mawson" (q.v.) for whom he was manager from 1868 to 1873. Morley went into partnership in Bradford with George Woodhouse (1829-1883) and later with his son George Herbert Woodhouse (born 1863) as "Morley & Woodhouse".

In 1878 a plan to build a new Wesleyan Chapel in Scarborough at the corner of Ramshill Road and Prince of Wales Road was postponed because of the volume of Wesleyan building in the town and a temporary wooden structure holding 100 people was erected instead. In 1884 an architectural competition was held for a design for a permanent church which was won by W.J.Morley of Bradford. The second prize went to John Hall of Scarborough (q.v.). South Cliff Wesleyan Church, built to Morley's design, was opened in July 1886.

References - (14), (44), (46), (57), (84), (85j), (92a), (92c), (94), (122), (123), (124).

NEWTON, John B.   **architect**
fl.Sc 1890

Scarborough work - none known

In the 1890 directory (only) for Scarborough John B.Newton is listed as an architect at 23, Commercial Street.

References - (36a).

55

NIXON, Robert   Scarborough harbour engineer
fl.Sc 1804-1824

Scarborough work - Harbour engineer (1804-24), brick lighthouse (1806).

Robert Nixon was appointed resident engineer to the Scarborough Harbour
Commissioners in 1804, in succession to Matthew Shout of Blyth. In 1806
the Commissioners instructed Nixon to erect a brick lighthouse, while in
1807 he was ordered to make a hole in the castle end of the pier to prevent
silt affecting Vincent's Pier. During his tenure, a western pier was built by
Barry & Hovington (1819-22). William Barry (1783-1838 q.v.) replaced
Nixon in 1824.
References - (93), (95), (114).

OATES, James   Scarborough architect
1869 (Scarborough) - post 1901

Scarborough work - domestic.

The son of Scarborough builder and contractor James Oates (born 1834
Scotland), James junior attended Scarborough School of Art where he was
amongst the prize winners in 1889 and 1890.
Between 1891 and 1901 Oates drew up plans for a variety of buildings in
Scarborough including houses, villas, warehouses and shops, mainly for
local builders including his father.
References - (14), (36a), (85j), (94).

OLIVER George Dale   Carlisle & Leeds architect
1851 (Sunderland) - 1928

Scarborough work – domestic.

The son of Thomas Oliver (q.v.), George Dale Oliver was articled to his
father and later was an assistant to George Edmund Street (1824-1881).
From 1876 Oliver practised from Carlisle and from Leeds. He became an
Associate of the Royal Institute of British Architects in 1877 and a Fellow
in 1892. From 1892 to 1919 he was County Architect for Cumbria and
most of his work was in Cumbria, Lancashire and Westmoreland.
Oliver designed alterations for Lady Sitwell's house "Woodend",
Scarborough in 1886 and did more work for her in 1891. Also in that year
he designed alterations and additions to "Park Lea", 10, Belmont Road,
Scarborough the house of his cousin, Dr Frederick Dale.
References - (14), (36a), (44), (54), (92d), (92i), (94), (101), (122), (123).

OLIVER Thomas　　　　　　**Sunderland & Newcastle architect**
1824 (Newcastle on Tyne) - 1902 (Jesmond)

Scarborough work - design for a Congregational Church. (1857).

In 1857 Thomas Oliver, the father of George Dale Oliver (q.v.), won an architectural competition for a new Congregational Church for Scarborough. The "Builder" reported that Oliver's design had been accepted for a new Church and Schools which were proposed for the North Cliff. The design was in a Venetian Gothic Style with alternate bands of coloured brickwork and terracotta enrichments and dressings'. The Scarborough Gazette in 1856 impressed the need for this church because of increasing resident population of the North Cliff, the increasing numbers of summer visitors and the "unattractive situation and buried position" of the Old Meeting House. It was hoped that there would be a generous response to an appeal for money, but presumably because of lack of funds the church seems not to have been built. The Old Meeting House was replaced by Eastborough Congregational Church designed by "Paull & Robinson" (q.v.) in 1869.
References - (14), (18), (26), (44), (57).

OUTHETT, John　　　　　　　　　**civil engineer**
fl.Sc. 1826-27

Scarborough work - Spa Bridge (1826-27).

In November 1826 a Mr Cattle of York promoted the Scarborough Cliff Bridge Company, to build a bridge connecting "The Cliff" i.e. St Nicholas' Cliff, Scarborough to the Spa to obviate the steep descent from the town to the Spa. It was estimated that the cost would be £4,500 to be raised in the form of £5 shares. Income for investors would come from charging tolls. The Yorkshire Gazette stated that Mr Outhwaite (sic) had been appointed engineer to the Company. In all later reports the same newspaper named the engineer as Mr John Outhett.
The foundation stone of the bridge was laid on 29th of November 1826, the Low Moor Iron Works manufactured the ironwork and the builders were "Messrs Stead, Snowden and Buckley" of York. There were complaints that work was progressing slowly and also that Mr Outhett, who was paid a fee of £200 exclusive of travelling expenses, was absent from site. Nonetheless the bridge was completed, although at a much greater cost, met by the issue of more shares. Scarborough Spa Bridge was opened on the 21st of July 1827 with a grand opening ceremony.
References - (85m), (95), (118).

PALEY & AUSTIN   **Lancaster architects' firm**
Edward Graham Paley (1823 Easingwold - 1895)
Hubert James Austin (1841 Co. Durham - 1915)

Scarborough work - St James Mission Chapel, Seamer Lane (1883), enlarged to become St James Church (1894), All Saints' Vicarage, Falsgrave Rd (1891), conversion of 17, 18, & 19, Falsgrave Rd to one house (1891).

Edward Graham Paley was a pupil of his brother-in-law Edmund Sharpe of Lancaster (1809-1877) and his partner from 1845 to 1851. In 1867 Paley was responsible for the Royal Albert Asylum in Lancaster and the next year he took Hubert James Austin as a partner forming the firm of "Paley & Austin". Both partners were sons of clergymen and specialised in building new churches and restoring old ones, especially in the North of England.
In Scarborough "Paley and Austin" designed St James Mission Chapel, Seamer Lane, built in 1883. They later designed enlargements to the building in 1893-4 to hold 350 people, electric lighting was installed and it was consecrated by the Archbishop of York in July 1894 as St James Church. The firm also designed a vicarage for Rev R.B.Borthwick, Vicar of All Saints' Church, Falsgrave.
Edward Paley, who was a founder of the British Archaeological Society in Lancaster (1844), died of typhoid on the 23rd of January 1895.
Hubert Austin died in 1915.
References - (14), (18), (21), (25), (44), (46), (54), (57), (85j), (92a), (92b), (92c), (94), (96), (97), (105).

PAULL & ROBINSON   **Manchester architects' firm**
Henry John Paull (1831 Worcester - 1888)
George Thomas Robinson (1827/8 - 1897)

Scarborough work - Congregational Church, Eastborough (1869).

"Paull & Robinson" was a Manchester firm of architects formed about 1868 with the partnership of H.P.Paull and G.T.Robinson and most of their work was in Lancashire.
In 1868 they were invited to Scarborough to re-model the old Independent Chapel in St Sepulchre Street (also known as The Old Meeting House). The scheme that "Paull & Robinson" adopted was virtually a re-building of the church providing frontages on both Eastborough and St Sepulchre Street. When the church was opened in 1869 its name was changed to Congregational Church "to encourage religious unity"
References - (14), (44), (85j), (92e), (101).

PAXTON, Sir Joseph   **landscape gardener & architect**
1801/3 - 1865

Scarborough work - Spa Grand Hall & gardens (1857 destroyed by fire 1876), Spa Observation Tower (1860 demolished 1923), (layout of) Weaponness Estate (1862).

Joseph Paxton began his career as a landscape gardener and produced a magazine of botany and a register of flowering plants (1834-49). He became superintendent of gardens for the Duke of Devonshire at Chatsworth (Derbyshire) where he designed a glass and iron conservatory (1836-40). He used this as the model for a building for the Great Exhibition of 1851 which was later re-erected as Crystal Palace at Sydenham. As an architect Paxton worked with his son-in-law George Henry Stokes (1827/8-1874) and together they designed Mentmore for Baron M.A.de Rothschild.

In 1857 the Scarborough Cliff Bridge Company invited Paxton to draw up plans for further developments at the Spa to include a new music hall, an observation tower and a bandstand. Paxton, assisted by his son-in-law, also drew up plans to landscape the steep land behind the Spa. At the same time John Barry (1803-66 q.v.) and his son designed and built a new carriage drive to Paxton's music hall and an extension to the Spa Promenade with an enlarged sea wall.

In 1863 Scarborough Corporation asked Sir Joseph Paxton to draw up plans to lay out and develop the land below Oliver's Mount known as the Weaponness Estate. Paxton's layout was accepted, access to the area was improved by the erection of the Ramsdale (Valley) Bridge in 1865 and plots on the estate were sold by auction in 1869 for the erection of villas.

In 1864 G.H.Stokes designed a new entrance to the Spa and the following year his plans for a glass and iron Winter Garden in the Spa grounds were on display at Theakston's Library in Scarborough but they were never adopted.

References - (18), (40), (44), (46), (54), (76), (85j), (92a), (92b), (94), (104), (106), (108), (118).

PEACOCK, Godfrey   **Scarborough architect**
1853 (Scarborough) - 1879 (Scarborough)

Scarborough work - Primitive Methodist Chapel, St John's Rd, Falsgrave (1880, demolished 1983).

Godfrey Peacock was son of the building contractor William Peacock (1826-93) and was articled to the architect Charles Bury (q.v.).

Peacock completed his articles and, having set up on his own, his first design was for a new Primitive Methodist Chapel in St John's Road. Unfortunately Peacock died in August 1879 aged 26 just when construction of the building was beginning. Charles Bury then took over completion of the chapel.

References - (85j), (120).

PENTY Walter Green   **York & Scarborough architect**
1853 (York) - 1902

Scarborough work – housing.
see also "Penty & Penty"

Walter Green Penty, a pupil of the York City engineer George Styan (q.v.), set up in independent practice in York in 1873.
In Scarborough, between 1882 and 1885, W.G.Penty designed 67 houses and cottages in the Sidney, Stanley and Sandringham streets area and the associated roads and drains. A possible association with the Scarborough architect John Petch (1819-97 q.v.) is suggested by an advertisement for tenders in 1882 which states that plans for the drainage scheme may be had from either architect.
Walter Penty had an office in Huntriss Row, Scarborough from 1897 until his death in 1902.

References - (14), (36a), (44), (85j), (92c), (94).

PENTY & PENTY   **York & Scarborough architects' firm**
Walter Green Penty (1853 - 1902)
Arthur Joseph Penty (1875 - 1937)

Scarborough work – "Dunollie", Filey Rd (1901).

In 1898 Walter Penty (q.v.) took his son Arthur Joseph Penty into partnership becoming "Penty & Penty" with offices in York and at 24 Huntriss Row, Scarborough.
In Scarborough in 1901, the firm designed the villa "Dunollie" on Filey Road for the York solicitor, Mr John Henry Turner.

References - (14), (36a), (44), (46), (85k), (92c), (94), (102), (122), (123), (124).

PETCH, David　　　　　　　　　　　　　　　**Scarborough architect**
1833 (West Heslerton) - 1888 (Scarborough)

Scarborough work – "Langford" and "Weston House", Westwood (1863), Seamer Rd Wesleyan Chapel (1878), Primitive Methodist school and chapel rooms. Gladstone Rd (1880), rebuilding of the Plough Inn, St Thomas St and the Star and Garter in Falsgrave (both 1881), Masonic Lodge. St Nicholas Cliff (conversion 1884).

David Petch was a younger brother of the architect John Petch (1819-1897 q.v.) who he joined in Scarborough when a young boy. David became an architect and the two brothers went into partnership as "J.& D.Petch" (q.v.) from about 1858 to 1870.　From 1871 onwards, the brothers had independent practices.

Besides designing many villas and houses, David Petch also designed the new Wesleyan Chapel. Seamer Road Falsgrave (1878) and a school and chapel rooms in Gladstone Road for the Primitive Methodist Connection (1880). He was involved in the rebuilding of the Plough Inn. St Thomas Street and the Star and Garter in Falsgrave (both 1881).　One of David Petch's later works was a design to convert a house. 14. St Nicholas Cliff. to become new Masonic premises (1884).

Two of David Petch's sons, James born 1858 (q.v.) and David born 1864 (q.v.), also became architects and in the late 1880s son David joined his father's practice.

David Petch died of a ruptured aortic aneurysm on the 27th of November 1888 aged 55.

References - (9), (14), (36a), (85j), (94), (120).

PETCH, David　　　　　　　　　　　　　　　**Scarborough architect**
1864 (Scarborough) -

Scarborough work - domestic

David Petch was the younger son of Scarborough architect David Petch (1833-88 q.v.) by whom he was presumably trained.

From 1895 he had his own practice in Scarborough designing houses and being involved with domestic additions and alterations.　He continued practice well into the 20th century.

References - (14), (36a), (94).

PETCH, Harry Scarborough architect
1875 (Scarborough) - 1943 (Ambleside)

Scarborough work – see "John Petch & Son".

Harry Petch was the son of Scarborough architect John Petch junior (born 1840 q.v.). He joined his father's practice about 1908 as a partner forming the firm of "John Petch & Son" (q.v.).
After his father's death, Harry continued the practice at 12, Valley Bridge Parade, maintaining the name "John Petch & Son".
Harry Petch died in 1943 while visiting his son in Ambleside.
References - (9), (14), (36a), (85k).

PETCH, James Scarborough architect
1858 (Scarborough) - post 1921

Scarborough work - domestic, North Side Cinema, North Marine Rd (1912).

James Petch was the elder son of Scarborough architect David Petch (1833-1888 q.v.) by whom he was presumably trained. From 1885 to about 1921 he had a practice in Scarborough designing many houses and being involved with domestic additions and alterations. In 1912 he designed a cinema (now the Hollywood Plaza) in North Marine Road for Mr R.Webb to which he added a balcony two years later.
References - (14), (36a), (85k), (94).

PETCH, John Scarborough architect
1819 (West Heslerton) - 1897 (Scarborough)

Scarborough work - Town Hall, St Nicholas St, repairs (1846), St Thomas Church, East Sandside, enlargement (1859), Bar Church Sunday School (1862), Bar Congregational Church enlargement (1873), Wesleyan Chapel, Scalby (1874), Circus St Thomas St (1876), Scarborough Cricket Club Refreshment Room, North Marine Rd (1878), Wheatcroft Congregational Mission Rooms (1879), Scarborough Aquarium, new entrance, baths offices etc. (1883-4), Rotunda Museum enlargement (1885), South Cliff Lawn Tennis grounds and pavilion (1885), Belvedere estate, Esplanade (1881-93).

John Petch was the eldest of several brothers born in West Heslerton (Yorks.) who all moved to Scarborough to become architects, surveyors or builders. John Petch was apprenticed to the Scarborough building contractor John Barry (1803-1866 q.v.) in 1832. Together with his brother Joseph Petch (q.v.), John worked in Scotland where Barry had several contracts including the breakwater at Arbroath for which John Petch was resident engineer (1842).

On returning to Scarborough Petch set up as an architect in the mid 1840s and one of his earliest jobs was for the Corporation to survey and repair the old Town Hall in St Nicholas Street which was in a much decayed state from the roof downwards (1846). Petch designed the Royal Crescent Hotel in Filey (1853) and a school in Muston (1855) but most of his work was in the growing town of Scarborough.

John Petch took his younger brother David (1833-88 q.v.) into partnership as "J.& D.Petch" (q.v.) from about 1858 to 1870. From 1871 onwards, the brothers had independent practices.

In the 1871 census John Petch described himself as "architect, 70 employees and labourers" suggesting that he also had a significant business as a contractor but in the 1881 census he described himself as "architect, farmer of 74 acres of land employing 2 labourers" at High Wheatcroft, Scarborough. John Petch worked both for private individuals such as the photographer Oliver Sarony (Circus, St Thomas Street 1876) and George Lord Beeforth (Belvedere Estate, Esplanade 1881-1893) and also for public bodies including the Scarborough School Board, Scarborough Aquarium Company, the South Cliff Tramway Company and Messrs Marshall & Snelgrove.

As well as running a very active architectural practice from his offices in Bar Street almost to his death, John Petch was for 27 years a Scarborough Councillor until 1889 when he was elected an alderman.

John Petch died in October 1897 at High Wheatcroft, South Cliff.

References - (9), (14), (36a), (43), (46), (85j), (92c), (94), (111).

PETCH, John (junior)   **Scarborough architect**
1840 (West Heslerton) -

Scarborough work - domestic.

John Petch was the nephew of the Scarborough architect John Petch (1819-1897 q.v.). According to the reminiscences of the elder John, the younger John was for many years his chief assistant as an architect.

From at least 1890 until about 1908 John junior was in independent practice in Scarborough and designed many villas and houses in Scarborough mostly on the south cliff.

His son Harry (q.v.) joined him about 1908 forming the firm of "John Petch & Son" (q.v.).

References - (9), (14), (36a), (94).

63

PETCH, John & Son   Scarborough architects' firm
John Petch (1840 -)
Harry Petch (1875 - 1943)
fl. 1908 – 1937

Scarborough work – "Wheatcroft Towers", Filey Rd (1908), St Edward's RC Church Avenue Victoria (1913).

John Petch, junior, (q.v.) took his son Harry into practice about 1908 as "John Petch & Son". They were responsible for several houses and villas in the south cliff area including "Wheatcroft Towers", Filey Road (1908). They designed the new Roman Catholic Church of St Edward in Avenue Victoria, the foundation stone for which was laid by the Bishop of Middlesborough in 1912.
After his father's death, Harry continued the practice at 12, Valley Bridge Parade maintaining the name "John Petch & Son".
References - (36a), (96).

PETCH, John Caleb   Scarborough architect
1853 (North Frodingham Yorks) - 1921 (Scarborough)

Scarborough work - Hydropathic Establishment, West Bank, now "Green Gables" (1889), New Exhibition Hall, Foreshore (1895 destroyed by fire 1975), Friarage Board School (1896), parsonage for Holy Trinity Church, 10, Oriel Crescent (1896), new frontage for the YMCA, 82, Westborough (1896), "Seaman's Institute", Sandside (1897), Model Lodging House, William St (1897), re-building 'Co-op' premises, 137, Victoria Rd (1897), Congregational Church, Manor Rd (1898), Primitive Methodist Chapel, Seamer Rd (1904), Baptist Church, Columbus Ravine (1911).

John Caleb Petch, son of joiner Joseph Petch, came to Scarborough in the 1860s. and by 1881 he was described as an 'architect assistant'. He became the son-in-law of the Borough Surveyor of Scarborough, Joseph Petch (q.v.). J.Caleb Petch was established in independent practice in Scarborough by the late 1880s. He trained at least two pupils in his office, T.C.Barker (q.v.) and H.A.Chapman (q.v.) and possibly his son Ernest Scott Petch (1885 - 1915) who became an architect working at H.M.Office of Works in Edinburgh but was killed in Gallipoli in the First World War.
An early design by J.C.Petch was the enormous Hydropathic Establishment at West Bank, Spring Hill, for Professor R.B.D.Wells, opened in 1889 (now Green Gables). It became so popular that two years later Petch designed extensive additions, including a recreation hall, built on newly acquired land. It was reopened in May 1891 as a limited liability company

with Petch as one of the directors.

J.Caleb Petch worked for Scarborough School Board on a variety of projects. In 1894 he won a competition for a design for the Friarage School which was chosen out of 37 entries and opened in 1896. John Woodall Woodall (1831-1905) chose J.C.Petch as the architect for his new exhibition hall on Foreshore (Olympia) erected for a fisheries and marine exhibition in 1895. Three years later Scarborough Corporation bought the hall. It was destroyed by fire in 1975.

J.Caleb Petch designed three churches in Scarborough - the New Congregational Church, corner of Manor Road and Gordon Street (1898), the New Primitive Methodist Chapel, Seamer Road, chosen by competition, (1904) and a new Baptist Church on Columbus Ravine (1911). He also did additions to the Jubilee Primitive Methodist Chapel in Aberdeen Walk (1900). He designed a "Seaman's Institute", Sandside for the Bishop of Hull (1897) and a parsonage for Holy Trinity Church, 10, Oriel Crescent, for the Rev. A.J.Shields (1896).

On the secular front he designed a new facade for the YMCA on Westborough (1896), additions to the Royal Theatre, St Thomas Street (1896) and produced plans for rebuilding the "Co-op" premises on Victoria Road (1897).

Petch was also very much involved with housing, designing numerous villas, houses and cottages. He designed the Model Lodging Houses and Institute in William Street accommodating 70 men (1897). One of his largest single requests was from the building contractors B.&W. Whalmsley for plans for Victoria Park, including roads, drains and almost 500 houses.

John Caleb Petch continued in practice at least until 1915 and died in September 1921.

References - (9), (14), (18), (36a), (44), (46), (84), (85j), (85k), (92c), (94), (101), (117), (122).

PETCH, Joseph   **Scarborough Borough Surveyor**
1821 (West Heslerton) - 1897 (Scarborough)

Scarborough work - Royal Albert Drive (1890), Marine Drive (1908).

Joseph Petch was one of several brothers born in West Heslerton (Yorks) who all moved to Scarborough to become architects, surveyors or builders. Joseph Petch was first apprenticed to John Barry (1803-66 q.v.) as a plasterer. In the early 1840s he went to Scotland with his brother John Petch (1819-97 q.v.) to assist Barry who was building a new breakwater at Arbroath.

On returning to Scarborough Joseph Petch set up as a bricklayer and builder but in 1857 he lost an arm in a brick-making machine and gave up his business to become an assistant to Scarborough's Borough Surveyor, Thomas Raper (q.v.). A legal dispute arose between Raper and the Council with the result that from 1869 Petch deputised for the Borough Surveyor although only on an assistant's salary. However, after 10 months the Council granted him a gratuity of £20 in respect of his extra responsibilities and Joseph Petch was then appointed Borough Surveyor, a post he held for 25 years.

Much of his work was involved with Borough improvements including housing, sewers and roads. During 1882 the eminent engineer Sir John Coode (q.v.) had been invited by Scarborough Council to draw up plans for improvements to the north cliff (including a road under Castle Cliff). Petch was required to adjust Coode's plans to reduce costs and his revisions were accepted by the Council. However, because of his other commitments in the town a series of resident engineers were appointed to supervise the work (see Whately Eliot and Robert Aytoun). The new road - Royal Albert Drive was formally opened by the HRH the Duke of Clarence in June 1890. As early as 1883 Joseph Petch had been preparing plans for a continuation of this, the then un-built Royal Albert Drive to reach as far as the harbour and Sir John Coode had presented a report and estimates on these plans. In November 1888 Joseph Petch again presented these plans as a "bird's eye view" entitled "Marine Drive, Seawall and Promenade". The project was finally approved by Scarborough Council in 1891, although work did not begin until 1896 and Marine Drive was finally opened in 1908 after Petch's death.

In 1892 Petch presented a paper on all the Public Works underway in Scarborough to the Incorporated Association of Municipal and County Engineers at their conference held in the town.

Joseph Petch retired in February 1896 and the Council awarded him a pension of £150 per annum. However, he died less than two years later in October 1897 at his home in Gladstone Street.

Joseph Petch's daughter Elizabeth (born 1851) married the architect John Caleb Petch (q.v.), while his eldest son William Petch (1850-1915) was an artist and art teacher becoming headmaster at Heeley Wesleyan Day School, Sheffield and his grandson Joseph B.Petch (born 1880) became a sculptor.

References - (9), (14), (36a), (58), (85j), (94), (100).

PETCH, J. & D.   **Scarborough architects' firm**
John Petch (1819-97)
David Petch (1833-88)
fl. 1858 - 1870

Scarborough work - Sarony's Studio, South Cliff (1858, demolished 1920s), Alexandra (now Clifton) Hotel, North Cliff (1864), Stamford House, Westwood (1864), Temperance Hall, North St (1868, demolished), St John's Rd Primitive Methodist Chapel (1869, demolished), Messrs Marshall & Snelgrove premises, St Nicholas St (Marshall House 1869).

The brothers John and David Petch went into partnership at 13, Bar Street about 1858 as "J.& D.Petch". One of their largest buildings, erected in 1858, was a photographic studio on South Cliff for the photographer and gallery owner Oliver Sarony (1819-79) which the "Photographic News" of the time said was more like a town hall than a studio. Other large buildings included the Alexandra Hotel (now the Clifton Hotel) on North Cliff built in 1864 and "Marshall House" - "Marshall & Snelgrove's" new premises in St Nicholas Street (1869). Their work also included churches, villas, including "Stamford House", Westwood (1864) and houses and shops particularly in the expanding South Cliff area in the 1860s. In 1870 they drew up plans for the enlargement of Scarborough Cemetery. After 1871 the brothers had independent practices.
References - (8), (36a), (57), (85j), (94), (112), (120).

PETCH, Thomas   **Scarborough builder & contractor**
1830 (West Heslerton) - 1905 (London)

Scarborough work - new Gaol Dean Rd (*1866), St Martin's Grammar School (*1870), St John's Rd Primitive Methodist Church (**1879).
* as contractor
** Petch & Fox contractors

Thomas Petch was one of several brothers born in West Heslerton (Yorks) who all moved to Scarborough to become architects, surveyors or builders. Thomas became a builder and contractor who designed and erected a considerable number of houses and cottages in the expanding town of Scarborough in the 1860s and 1870s. Larger building contracts included the new gaol designed by W.B.Stewart (q.v.) (1866) and St Martin's Grammar School designed by G.F.Bodley (q.v.) (1870).
In the late 1860s Thomas Petch went into partnership with builder and contractor Robert Fox (1830 -1904) and the partnership built many more Scarborough houses. In 1879 they were the contractors for the Primitive

Methodist Chapel, St John's Road, designed by G.Peacock (q.v.).
The partnership continued until Thomas Petch died in 1905 after a road
accident in London. His son W.T.Petch (q.v.) then took over the business.
References - (9), (14), (36a), (85j), (94), (120).

PETCH, William Thomas   Scarborough builder & contractor
1861 (Scarborough) - 1939 (Scarborough)

Scarborough work - St Columba's Church window tracery (*1928), St
Luke's Church, Scalby Rd (*1932), St Mark's Church, Newby (*1935)
* as contractor

William Thomas Petch was the son of builder and contractor Thomas Petch
(q.v.) who took over his father's business in Victoria Road after his death
in 1905. W.T.Petch continued the business into the 20th century and
amongst other work was responsible for St Luke's Church, Scalby Road
(1932) and St Mark's Church, Newby (1935). The company was the lessee
of Cloughton Quarries and W.T.Petch was a specialist in stone work and
responsible for the window tracery in St Columba's Church, Scarborough
(1928).
William Thomas Petch died at his home after a fall while adjusting
"blackout" at his Victoria Road works in December 1939.
References - (9), (14), (36a), (85k).

PRITCHETT, & Sons   Darlington & York architects' firm
fl.Sc. 1856

Scarborough work - two cemetery chapels, Dean Road (1856).

In 1856 the firm of "Pritchett & Sons" won an architectural competition for
the construction of two chapels at the new cemetery in Dean Road,
Scarborough. The firm specialised in the design of cemeteries and the
Scarborough design is ascribed to James Piggott Pritchett. However there
were two Pritchetts with this name - father (1789-1868) and son (1830-
1911) and either could have been the designer.
References - (26), (36a), (57), (92a), (92b), (92c), (101).

RAPER, Thomas   **Scarborough Borough Surveyor**
1833 (Guisborough) - post 1889
fl.Sc 1861-1870

Scarborough work - new Town Hall, courts and police station, Castle Road/St Thomas St (1869-70 closed 1965).

Thomas Raper came to Scarborough as a building inspector about 1860. By 1864 he is listed an architect and as such he prepared several plans for houses, shops and a warehouse. However, by 1867 he is listed as "borough surveyor and inspector of gas meters". In 1869 he was described as "the late borough surveyor" when he was brought before Scarborough magistrates for failing to deliver certain moneys owed to the Council (£62-4s-9d). In the following year Raper came under criticism at a public meeting concerning the cost of building the new Town Hall and he wrote a letter to the Scarborough Gazette defending his position. He pointed out that he had drawn up plans to convert the old gaol in Castle Road into a police station and magistrates and sessions court and some extra cost had been incurred when the original foundations were found to be poor being on the site of the old town moat. Further, half way through building Scarborough Corporation decided that this should also be the site of a new Town Hall with Corporation offices. New plans had to be made and much of the completed building work altered. This, he said, had been the cause of the increased the cost rather than any neglect on his part.

Thomas Raper left Scarborough to work as an architect and surveyor in Bedale and his post of Borough Surveyor was filled by Joseph Petch (1821-1897 q.v.)

References - (14), (36a), (85j), (94).

ROBSON, Edward Robert   **London architect/ judge**
1835 (Durham) - 1917 (London)

Scarborough work - (judge for competition for) Higher Grade (Westwood) School (1897).

Edward Robson became an Associate of the Royal Institute of British Architects in 1860 and a Fellow in 1864. He was architect to the Dean and Chapter of Durham (1858-64), to the Corporation of Liverpool (1864-71) and to the London School Board (1871-89). From 1884 to 1908 he was architect to Education Department for England, Wales & Scotland. He specialised in the architecture of school buildings and in 1874 published a book on the subject. It was in this capacity that he judged the designs submitted for Scarborough Higher Grade (Westwood) School. The competition drew entries from all parts of the country but Robson awarded first prize to the Scarborough firm of "Hall, Cooper and Davis" (q.v.).

Robson's other connection with Scarborough architects is that from 1883-1886 Frank Tugwell (q.v.) worked in his office in London. Robson proposed Tugwell, and Henry Hare (q.v.), another Scarborough born architect, as Associates of the Royal Institute of British Architects.

References - (44), (54), (57), (85j), (92a), (92b), (92e), (101), (122).

ROBSON, William   **Scarborough builder & architect**
1829 (Scarborough) - 1907

Scarborough work - housing.

William Robson became a builder and contractor in Castle Road, Scarborough and ran a flourishing business into the 20th century. In addition to his work as a builder he also designed numerous villas and houses mainly in the South Cliff area of Scarborough. William was a founder member of the Scarborough Master Builders' Association in 1891.

William Robson's son Thomas Robson (1860-1928), who attended Scarborough School of Art, also designed and built many houses on South Cliff.

References - (14), (36a), (85j), (94), (98).

ROPER, Frederick William   **London architect**
1840 (Bath) - 1910

Scarborough work – "Belvedere", Esplanade (1885).

Frederick Roper was articled to the Bath architect James Wilson (1816-1900) and became an Associate of the Royal Institute of British Architects in 1863. He set up in independent practice in London in 1869.

In Scarborough Roper designed the villa "Belvedere" on Esplanade for George Lord Beeforth (1823-1924) who at the time was proprietor of the "Doré Gallery" in London. This house was the centrepiece of the "Belvedere Estate" development (1881-93) for which John Petch (1819-93 q.v.) was the main architect.

Frederick Roper died on the 6th December 1910.

References - (14), (18), (27), (44), (46), (54), (57), (101), (102).

ROWNTREE, Fred London architect
1860 (Scarborough) -1927 (London)

Scarborough work – Sandside Coffee House, corner of Eastborough and Foreshore Rd (1882), "Riseborough" Weaponess Park (1898), "Roscoe Rooms" - adult school Roscoe St (1903), "Low Hall", Scalby (1904), School, Filey Rd (1909 now University of Hull Scarborough Campus) "The Nabs", Scalby Nabs (1912).
see also "Edeson & Rowntree" and "Stark & Rowntree".

Frederick Rowntree was the fourth son of John and Ann Rowntree, educated at Bootham School, York. He was articled to Scarborough architect Charles Bury (q.v.) and later to Edward Burgess (q.v.) of London. One of Rowntree's earliest projects in Scarborough was in 1882 when he replaced the clerk of works (J.J.Kay) during the building of William Rowntree's department store in Westborough to the design of Edward Burgess. Also in this year Rowntree designed a coffee house on the corner of Eastborough and Foreshore Road for the Scarborough Coffee House Co.
Fred Rowntree went into partnership in Scarborough with Charles Edeson (q.v.) until about 1890 as "Edeson & Rowntree" (q.v.) and in 1891 Rowntree entered partnership with the Glasgow architect Malcolm Stark as "Stark & Rowntree" (q.v.).
By 1904 Fred Rowntree had settled in London where he spent the rest of his professional life, later taking his sons, Douglas Woodville and Colin, into partnership to form the firm of "F.Rowntree & Sons" with a branch office in York.
However, Fred Rowntree continued doing work for the Rowntree Family in and around Scarborough. He designed villas for members of the family including – "Riseborough", Scarborough for George Rowntree (1898); "Cherry Hill", Bransby for O.Rowntree (1903); "Low Hall", Scalby for J. W.Rowntree (1904); "The Nabs" at Scalby Nabs for J.H.Rowntree (1912) and the "Manor House", at Langdale End for Mrs J.W.Rowntree (1924). He also designed "The Roscoe Rooms" - an adult school in Roscoe Street, Scarborough (1903) and a large school building with swimming baths and a dining hall on Filey Road for Edward A.Cooper MA, now part of Scarborough Campus of Hull University (1909).
Beyond Scarborough, Fred Rowntree was prolific. He was responsible for many Quaker Meeting Houses in Great Britain, considerable school work in York, including new class rooms for his old school, and in 1913 he designed the West China Union University at Chengdu, China.
Frederick Rowntree died in London in 1927, aged 66, after an operation.
References - (1), (14), (36a), (44), (46), (68), (82), (85j), (85k), (92a), (92c), (92g), (94), (100), (101), (119), (122), (123), (124).

RUNTON & BARRY   Scarborough & Hull architects' firm
Percy Runton (1874-1947)
William Ernest Barry (1867-1924)
fl. c.1896-1918

Scarborough work - Poor Law Offices, Dean Rd (1900), "Hertford House", Filey Rd (1903).

From about 1896 until 1918 W.E.Barry (q.v.) was in partnership with the Hull architect Percy Runton as "Runton and Barry". Besides offices in Hull, the partners also worked from Huntriss Row, Scarborough until about 1910. In Scarborough, the "Runton & Barry" worked for the Board of Guardians and had a domestic practice which included the design of "Hertford House", Filey Road (1903) for Mrs Radcliffe.
From 1910 until 1918 the practice was conducted only from Hull, where the partners designed many shops and business premises including Ferens Homes and Reckett's Alms Houses. The firm also specialised in the design of garden suburbs such as the Garden Village, with 600 houses, opened in 1908 and the Anlaby Park Estate, both in Hull. In 1918 Runton moved to Bradford and Barry moved to Dorset.
References – (36a), (36d), (44), (86), (92c), (94), (101), (122), (123), (124).

RUSSELL & COOPER   London architects' firm
Samuel Bridgeman Russell (1864 - 1955)
Thomas Edwin Cooper (1874 - 1942)
fl. 1905-1912

Scarborough work - Printing works extensions (1910).

From 1905 to 1912 Thomas Edwin Cooper (q.v.) was in partnership with Samuel Bridgemen Russell in London as "Russell & Cooper".
In Scarborough "Russell & Cooper" drew up plans for additions to Meredith T.Whittaker's Printing Works in Aberdeen Walk in 1910.
References – (44), (92a), (92c), (94), (101), (122), (123), (124).

SANDERSON, Louis Norman   Scarborough architect
1881 (Scarborough) - post 1939

Scarborough work – "Wedgwood Court" (1912), Marks & Spencer's premises, 9-10, Westborough (1925).

Louis Sanderson was a prize winning student at Scarborough School of Art from 1895 to 1900. From 1908 until at least 1939 he ran an architectural practice in Scarborough where he designed "Wedgwood Court" (1912) and new premises for "Marks & Spenser" at 9-10, Westborough. At nearby Ganton he designed the Golf Club House (1912) and at Whitby the Royal Hotel (1920).

References – (14), (36a), (85j), (94), (101), (122), (123), (124).

SEDDING, John Dando   **architect**
1838 (Eton) - 1891 (Somerset)

Scarborough work – "Wheatcroft Cliff" (Holbeck Hall Hotel) (1878, slid into the sea 1993).

John Dando Sedding worked in the office of George Edmund Street (1824-1881) becoming a Fellow of the Royal Institute of British Architects in 1874 and was in practice with his brother Edmund Sedding. J.D.Sedding was known for his exquisite ornamental detail in churches and other buildings.
In 1878 J.D.Sedding exhibited a design at the Royal Academy in London – "Wheatcroft", Scarborough'. This was the house "Wheatcroft Cliff" that he designed for Scarborough businessman George Alderson Smith. The building, later known as the Holbeck Hall Hotel, slid into the sea in 1993.

References - (27), (44), (50), (54), (92b), (101).

SHARP, Richard Hey   **York architect**
1793-1853 (Heyworth Moor)

Scarborough work - Rotunda Museum (1829), Trinity House, St Sepulchre St (1832).

Richard Hey Sharp was a pupil of the York architect Peter Atkinson (jun.) (q.v.) with whom he went into partnership in 1819 after studying in Italy and Greece. In 1827 he set up in independent practice in York but four years later he took into partnership his younger brother Samuel (1808-74) who was also a pupil of Atkinson.
Among Richard Sharp's works were the Assembly Rooms at Hull (1830-34) - now the New Theatre, the rebuilding of St Saviour's Church at York (1844-1845) and St Mary's Church at Roecliffe (1845).
In Scarborough, R.H.Sharp, in collaboration with the geologist William Smith, designed the Rotunda as a purpose built museum for the Scarborough Philosophical Society, founded in 1827. The Rotunda was opened in 1829 and the wings were added in 1861. Sharp also designed "Trinity House" in St Sepulchre Street, a home for "worn out mariners", to

replace an older hospital on the site. The new "Trinity House" was opened in 1832.

Also in Scarborough R.H.Sharp was commissioned to prepare plans for laying out the "Valley". Part of his layout, including the Crescent, was executed in the 1830s and 1840s. In 1837 "R.H.& S.Sharp" prepared plans for a new Spa Building in Scarborough and although accepted by the Spa Committee it was a design by Henry Wyatt (q.v.) that was actually erected.
References - (21), (26), (36b), (44), (73), (85m), (92a), (92c), (104), (118).

SHIELDS, Thomas, W.W.   Greenwich civil engineer
1821 (Ireland) -

Scarborough work - Widening of Spa Bridge (1880).

After the Scarborough Spa buildings burnt down in 1876 the opportunity was taken, not only to rebuild them to the design of "Verity & Hunt" (q.v.), but also to widen the Cliff Bridge, originally built in 1826 by John Outhett (q.v.). Thomas W.W.Shields of Greenwich was the civil engineer responsible for this work and also for widening two pathways from the bridge, one to the Spa and one to the South Cliff. The Spa and bridge were re-opened in August 1880 with great ceremony with Thomas Shields amongst the leaders of the procession.
References - (14), (49), (85j).

SIMPSON, James   Leeds architect
1792 - 1864 (Leeds)

Scarborough work - Queen St Wesleyan Chapel, (1840 destroyed by fire 1915).

James Simpson settled in Leeds about 1822 and specialised in the design of non-conformist chapels with classical facades, mostly in that City.

In Scarborough, Simpson designed a Wesleyan Chapel in Queen Street which was built 1839-40 and described as the largest dissenting place of worship in the town. It was destroyed by fire in 1915.
References - (26), (44), (92a), (92b), (92c), (111).

SIMPSON, Thomas   Nottingham architect
fl.Sc 1860

Scarborough work - United Methodist Free Church (Claremont Chapel), Castle Rd (1860).

Thomas Simpson designed the United Methodist Free Church, Castle Road

(Claremont Chapel) which was opened on the 1st November 1860. The Scarborough Gazette described the Grecian style building as "beautiful and commodious". Beneath the chapel Simpson had included a school with six classrooms. The body of the chapel was lit by four "star-lights" each light containing 54 (gas) burners said to be the only specimens of their kind in Scarborough.

References - (44), (46), (57), (85j), (92a).

STARK & ROWNTREE   **Glasgow architects' firm**
Malcolm Stark (1855 -)
Fred Rowntree (1860-1927)
fl. 1891-1900

Scarborough work - Friends' Meeting House, York Place (1894 demolished 1990), adult school, St Sepulchre St (1894), Temperance Hall, Scalby (1894), school gymnasium (1894), John Rowntree & Sons Cafe, 11, Westborough (1896).

The Scottish architect Malcolm Stark and Fred Rowntree (q.v.) were in partnership in Glasgow from 1891 to 1900 as "Stark & Rowntree".
Although based in Scotland they did much work for the Rowntree families in Scarborough. In particular "Stark & Rowntree" were responsible for the conversion of an ironmonger's premises to become John Rowntree & Sons's Westborough Cafe (1896), the interior decoration being by "George Walton & Co." (George Walton 1867-1933). "Stark & Rowntree" also worked for William Rowntree & Sons designing additions to their Department Store at 33-39, Westborough. The partners designed the Friends Meeting House in York Place (opened 1894), an adult school in St Sepulchre Street (1894) and a Temperance Hall at Scalby, near Scarborough (1894) - now the Methodist Hall. Also in 1894 they designed a gymnasium for Miss Maria Woodhead's School for Ladies at the "Westlands", Westbourne Grove.

References – (14), (85k), (94), (101), (119).

STEWART, William Baldwin   **Scarborough architect**
1832 (London) - post 1870
fl.Sc 1860 - 70

Scarborough work - Northern Sea Bathing Infirmary, Foreshore (1860), Jubilee Chapel, Aberdeen Walk (1861, demolished 1966), Methodist Chapel, Westborough (1862), Lancasterian Schools, High Tollergate (1862), Wheelhouse and Buckle Dwellings (1865 demolished), Amicable Society's School (c.1865), "The Towers", 170, Castle Rd (1866), New

Borough Gaol, Dean Rd (1866) and Refreshment Rooms, Grand Hotel (1871).

William Baldwin Stewart came to Scarborough from London about 1860 as the winning competitor for a design for the Northern Sea Bathing Infirmary. Between 1854 and 1857 he worked in New York where his son was born. Most of his known work is in Scarborough, although he was responsible for All Saints Church at Muston (1863-4) and the now demolished Bridlington Quay (Alexandra) Hotel at Bridlington (1863-4). Stewart seems to have run a single-handed practice in Scarborough although a letter dated 1869 is headed "W.B. & V. Stewart", 4, Sydney Place while a newspaper article in 1870 refers to "Messrs Stewart". The 1871 census for Scarborough does not include W.B Stewart but there are listed a Victor Stewart born 1819 in Marylebone and a W.B.Stewart junior born in 1856 in New York. Victor Stewart was listed as an architect in New York in 1858 at the address W.B.Stewart previously had.

From 1870 to 1871 Stewart was in partnership with his assistant, C.A.Bury (q.v.) as "Stewart & Bury" after which Stewart does no further work in Scarborough.

W.B. Stewart's buildings ranged from churches, almshouses and schools to huge hotels. Designs for several of Stewart's buildings were chosen by national and local competitions including the Westborough Methodist Chapel where 30 other designs were submitted. His designs for the Lancasterian Schools and schools for the Amicable Society were chosen locally by unanimous decisions of the judges. His design for the Bridlington hotel was also chosen in a competition although his design for a Mechanics' Institute at Bolton only gained second place.

References - (6), (14), (36a), (46), (49), (57), (80), (85j), (85k), (92a) (92c), (94), (96), (106), (116) (125).

STEWART & BURY   **Scarborough architects' firm**
William Baldwin Stewart (1832-post 1870)
Charles Augustus Bury (1846-post 1885)
fl.Sc. 1870 - 1873

Scarborough work – Pavilion Hotel (1870 demolished 1973), Londesborough Rooms (Theatre) 1871, Central Board School, Trafalgar St West (1873, demolished), Long Westgate Board School (a conversion 1873), South Cliff Tramway (1875).

After practising alone in Scarborough from about 1860, W.B.Stewart (q.v.) took his assistant, C.A.Bury (q.v.), into partnership in 1870 as " Stewart & Bury". In the following year Bury paid Stewart £250 and took over the practice, the partnership being dissolved. However the name "Stewart & Bury" continued to be used by Bury for a further two years.

"Stewart & Bury" were responsible for the "Pavilion Estate", which included the Pavilion Hotel (1870) for John Skelton and the Londesborough Rooms on Westborough (1871) which became the Londesborough Theatre. The South Cliff Tramway Company appointed "Stewart & Bury" as their architects, their engineer being W. Harrington Lucas (q.v.).

References – (14), (36a), (49), (85j), (92a), (94).

STYAN, George & Henry   **York architects**
George Styan 1824 (York) -
Henry Styan

Scarborough work - Dean Rd Workhouse (1859).

George and Henry Styan were York architects commissioned by Scarborough Poor Law Guardians to design a new workhouse which was built in Dean Road under the Styans' supervision (1859-60). Henry Styan then moved to Manchester and George Styan designed extensions to Scarborough workhouse in 1864 and 1868.

George Styan later became City Surveyor of York.

References - (14), (44), (92a), (92c), (92e), (94), (106).

TAYLOR, Alexander   **Scarborough Borough Surveyor**
1823 (Ireland) - 1866 (Stockport)
fl.Sc 1859-1864

Scarborough work - Road and sewerage improvements, street furniture (1859-64).

From about 1859 Alexander Taylor was surveyor to the Scarborough Improvement Commissioners and was also Borough Surveyor. In these roles he planned and carried out improvement to sewerage on the north side of town, building a covered tube out to sea (1859) and in 1862 he was experimenting with methods of deodorising night soil and sewage. He planned and supervised improvements to town roads and in 1862 proposed plans for enlarging the harbour west pier. He designed, amongst other things, a metal weigh house, gas lamp, drinking fountain and pan all combined in one structure (1859). In 1864 Taylor was involved with plans for a new Borough Gaol designed by W. Baldwin Stewart (q.v.) and opened in 1866.

Alexander Taylor died in April 1866 and in the next month Scarborough

Council was asked for financial support to the widow and family of the late Borough Surveyor.
References - (85j).

THOMPSON, John   **Scarborough builder**
1798 (Scarborough) - post 1855

Scarborough work - National Schools, Queen St (Girls 1836 demolished 1859), (Boys 1837 demolished 1859).

In 1835 a National School for Scarborough was proposed but there were no funds available for this project. In 1836 a local builder, John Thompson, offered to erect a building for 100 children. A school for girls was completed in 1836 and one for boys in 1837, by which time an endowment of £300 had been made to the schools benefit by Lord Feversham.
The schools were demolished in 1859 when new buildings were erected to the design of Ewan Christian (q.v.).
References - (5), (9), (14), (36a), (111).

TUGWELL, Frank Alfred   **Scarborough architect**
1862 (Scarborough) - 1940 (Scarborough)

Scarborough work - additions to Albemarle Hotel, Westborough (1895), alterations to the Royal Hotel (1895), rebuilding of Newcastle Packet Inn (1898), "Brookholme", Holbeck Hill, (1899), alterations to the Leeds Hotel, West Sandgate (1900), alterations to Durham Hotel, North Marine Road (1900), alterations to the Royal Vaults, Market St (1900), Nurses Home, Scarborough Hospital (1900), Manor Rd Cemetery Lodge and Chapel (1901), Wesleyan Church, Hoxton Road (1905), alterations to "Hole in Wall" public house (1905).
see also "Barry & Tugwell", "Hall & Tugwell" and "Tugwell, Messrs"

Frank Tugwell was the elder son of Scarborough hairdresser and councillor Alfred Tugwell. In 1879 Frank Tugwell was articled to John Hall (q.v.) and at the same time attended Scarborough School of Art where he was awarded a Government Certificate in 1883. Tugwell then entered the London office of E.R.Robson (q.v.) and in 1886 and became an Associate of the Royal Institute of British Architects, Robson being one of his proposers.
Frank Tugwell returned to Scarborough and rejoined John Hall to form the firm "Hall and Tugwell" (q.v.) which lasted until 1894. Tugwell had a brief association with William Ernest Barry (q.v.) in 1897/98 as "Barry & Tugwell" (q.v.) and, also in 1898, with his younger brother Sydney

Tugwell (q.v.), see "Messrs Tugwell" (q.v.).

Thereafter Frank Tugwell practiced independently in Scarborough where he did much domestic work and designed many fine villas particularly on Holbeck Hill including "Brookholme" for Mrs E.Brooke (1899). Another area in which he specialised was the renovation of Scarborough hotels and public houses based on experience gained with "Hall & Tugwell" (q.v.). Working for Scarborough Burial Board, Tugwell designed the Cemetery Chapel and stables on Manor Road (1901) with further additions in 1904.

After the First World War, which claimed the life of his son Geoffrey Arnold Tugwell (1893-1917), Frank Tugwell was the architect for the reconstruction of the Spa Grand Hall, Scarborough. His plans included what is now the Vitadome, although it was not built until 1931. His plan for a lift directly into Spa Grand Hall was never realised because of, amongst other things, objections from Esplanade residents about the proposed height of the upper station.

Frank Tugwell was active politically - he was made a magistrate in 1926; he was a Conservative member of the North Riding County Council (NRCC) from 1900 to 1928 and a committee member of NRCC's Higher Education Committee from 1903, being its chairman from 1929 to 1940. He was also a committee member of Scarborough School of Art to which he was a generous subscriber.

In 1901 Frank Tugwell was responsible for the re-building of the Theatre Royal in St Leonard's Place York originally built (1877-79) by George Styan (q.v.). He was later responsible for several other theatres including the internal construction of the Savoy Theatre, London in 1929 with Basil Ionides (1884-1950) as well as theatres in Harrogate and Manchester.

Frank Alfred Tugwell retired from architecture about 1935 and died in Scarborough on the 20th of March 1940, aged 78.

References - (14), (18), (31), (36a), (44), (46), (57), (85j), (89), (90), (92a), (92c), (94), (99), (101), (118), (122), (123), (124).

TUGWELL, Sydney   **Bournemouth architect**
1869 (Scarborough) - 1938 (Scarborough)

Scarborough work - none
see "Tugwell Messrs"

Sydney Tugwell, the younger son of Scarborough hairdresser and councillor Alfred Tugwell, studied at Scarborough School of Art. Here he won prizes in building construction and drawing (1885) and in advanced building construction, perspective, and architecture (1887). He trained as an architect in the London office of Norman Shaw (1831-1912) and was said to be influenced by the work of Edward J. May (q.v.), who was also a pupil of Norman Shaw. Tugwell became a Fellow of the Royal Institute of British Architects.

Sydney Tugwell briefly worked with his architect brother Frank Tugwell (q.v.) between 1896 and 1898 (see "Messrs Tugwell") but soon after moved to Bournemouth where he was at once involved with the completion of St Andrew's Church in 1899. In 1903 he designed a new spire for St Paul's Church Bournemouth, erected as a memorial to Queen Victoria and also designed the communion silver for the church. Sydney Tugwell continued his architectural practice at Richmond Chambers, Bournemouth into the 1930s and retired to Scarborough in 1937 where he died on the 23rd July 1938.

References - (10), (11), (14), (18), (44), (85d), (85e), (85j), (85k), (94), (101), (110), (122), (123), (124).

TUGWELL, Messrs   **Scarborough architects' firm**
Frank Tugwell (1862 - 1940)
Sydney Tugwell (1869 - 1938)
fl. 1896-1898

Scarborough work - rebuilding of Royal Hotel Stables (1897), St Martin's Church School, Royal Avenue (1898 demolished 1989), rebuilding Newcastle Packet Inn (1898), alterations to Albert Hotel, North Marine Rd (1898).

Frank Tugwell (q.v.) and his younger brother Sydney Tugwell (q.v.) worked together as "Messrs Tugwell" for about two years from 1896 to 1898. During this period they produced designs for houses and villas on South Cliff, were involved with alterations to a number of hotel and public houses. However, their main work together was the design of St Martin's Church School in Royal Avenue (1898).

References – (18), (31), (85j), (94).

VERITY & HUNT   **London architects**
Verity, Thomas (1837 Covent Garden -1891 London)
Hunt, George Henry (1851 Evesham - 1915 Evesham)

Scarborough work - Spa Buildings (1877-80).

Thomas Verity spent his early 20s in architects' offices firstly at the War Office and then at South Kensington Museum. In 1866 he was sent to Italy by the House of Lords Committee on Education to study Italian architecture and the uses of terracotta. He became a Fellow of the Royal Institute of British Architects in 1870 and in the same year went in to independent practice.

George Hunt studied architecture at the South Kensington School of Art and at the Royal Academy Schools (1871-78). He travelled in France, Italy and Switzerland studying architecture (1873-74) and began work with his architect father George Hunt of Evesham (1874-75) and then started practice on his own in 1875 becoming a Fellow of the Royal Institute of British Architects in 1891.

In 1876 a disastrous fire destroyed much of the Scarborough Spa buildings including the Grand Hall of 1858 by Joseph Paxton (q.v.), which had retained part of the "Gothic Pavilion" of 1839 by Henry Wyatt (q.v.). The Scarborough Cliff Bridge Company, owners of the Spa, sought the help of the secretary to the Royal Institute of British Architects, Mr F.P.Cockerill to set conditions for a competition to re-build the structure. Twenty-six designs were submitted from which Cockerill chose four and the company awarded first prize to Verity & Hunt and second prize to John Gibson & Son of Malton (q.v.). Work began in October 1877 and the new building was opened to the public in June 1879. Although contemporary Scarborough newspaper reports refer to "Verity & Hunt", it appears that they were close collaborators rather than formal partners. They exhibited their Scarborough Spa designs at the Royal Academy in London in 1881 under the name "Verity & Hunt" although it appears that it was Thomas Verity who made the major contribution to the design.

References - (3), (14), (18), (44), (49), (50), (54), (57), (85j), (89), (92a), (102), (104), (118).

WALTERS, Frederick Arthur   London architect
1850 (Brompton, Middlesex) - 1932

Scarborough work - Convent of the Dames de Marie, Queen St (1884).

Frederick Arthur Walters was articled to his architect father Frederick Page Walters for 3 years and studied at the Royal Academy Schools (1871). He worked in the office of "Goldie & Childs" for several years and became an Associate of the Royal Institute of British Architects in 1882. He practiced in London specialising in the design of Roman Catholic buildings.

In 1884 the Nuns of the Order of the Dames de Marie of Tollergate House, Scarborough had bought a site known as the Bowling Green in Queen Street for a new convent. F.A.Walters was chosen as architect and the main contractor was John Barry (1833-1910 q.v.). The convent was opened by the Roman Catholic Bishop of Middlesborough in 1886.

References - (14), (18), (44), (46), (54), 85j), (92a), (94), (101), (102).

WARWICK, Thomas   entrepreneur
fl.Sc 1898

Scarborough work - Warwick's Revolving Tower (1898, demolished 1906).

Thomas Warwick was the proprietor of "Warwick's Revolving Tower Company" which had obtained rights from the American designers of the tower to erect them as tourist attractions in England, the first being at Great Yarmouth (opened 9/7/1897).

Warwick visited Scarborough in 1897 and chose a site at the "Castle by the Sea" and commissioned the Scarborough firm of "Hall Cooper & Davis" (q.v.) as his architects. Although there was opposition to such a structure from townsfolk, the plans were approved and Warwick's Tower was opened on the 30th July 1898. Further towers were constructed at Morecambe (opened 1/6/1898) and at Douglas, Isle of Man (opened 2/6/1899) but was later moved to Cleethorpes (opened 21/6/1902).

In Scarborough, Warwick's Tower, locally called "the revolting tower", was so disliked that Mr Alfred Shuttleworth of "Red Court" bought it in 1906 and had it demolished.

References - (16a), (37), (39), (67), (85g), (85j), (89).

WATSON, William   **Wakefield architect**
1840 (Middlesborough) - 1901

Scarborough work - Falsgrave Board School, Falsgrave Rd/Sitwell St (1872), Wesleyan Sunday School, Queen St (1879).

William Watson was the son of Thomas Watson, a builder and joiner, who came to Scarborough with his family in the mid 1840s. Thomas was active in Scarborough as builder, joiner and lodging house proprietor at least until 1890.

William Watson trained as an architect and set up in practice in Wakefield.

In Scarborough he designed the Falsgrave Board School (1872) and a Sunday School built at the side of the Wesleyan Chapel in Queen Street (1879). In the vicinity of Scarborough he designed a new Wesleyan Chapel at nearby Harewood Dale (1880).

References - (14), (36a), (44), (73), (85j), (92a), (94), (101).

WHIPP, Thomas William   **Scarborough architect**
1880 (Scarborough) - 1950 (Scarborough)

Scarborough work – housing, Scarborough Historical Pageant (1912).

The son of a Scarborough wheelwright, Thomas Whipp studied at Scarborough School of Art where he was amongst the prize winning students from 1894 to 1899. Whipp worked for a period in the Architect's Department of London County Council and having completed his articles became an Associate of the Royal Institute of British Architects in 1902.

Whipp set up his own practice in York Place, Scarborough but soon moved to 15, Valley Bridge Parade, an office he maintained until his death, the only gap being a period in the Royal Naval Air Service in the First World War.

Thomas Whipp was architect to the Scarborough Historical Pageant of 1912, responsible for, amongst other things, structures such as the grandstands. After the First World War, both as an architect and surveyor, he was involved in much of the post war housing and new estates in Scarborough. In the 1920s and 1930s he lectured on building construction at Evening Classes in the Town and in the Second World War was a panel assessor for war damage.

Two drawings by Whipp of decorative wrought iron gates in Scarborough are to be found in Rowntree's "The History of Scarborough".

A prominent freemason, Thomas William Whipp died on the 28th June 1950.

References - (14), (36a), (44), (85j), (94), (99), (101), (122), (123), (124).

WILLIAMS, James   **Government architect/surveyor**
1822   (Chelsea) - 1892

Scarborough work – GPO, Huntriss Row (now Royal Bank of Scotland) (1881).

James Williams was a surveyor working for Her Majesty's Office of Works in Whitehall in 1879 when it was decided to build a new General Post Office (GPO) in Scarborough. Williams designed a classical style building for a site in Huntriss Row which was opened to the public in April 1881. The construction contract went to a York builder Robert Weatherley.

References - (14), (85j), (92c), (101).

WRIGHT, Joseph   **Hull architect**
1818 (Hessle) - 1885

Scarborough work - Methodist Chapel, St Sepulchre St (1865, demolished 1967).

Joseph Wright, a pupil of Cuthbert Brodrick (q.v.), was an active Primitive Methodist. Wright designed numerous chapels in Hull, the East Riding of Yorkshire and North Lincolnshire over a twenty year period from the late 1850s.
In Scarborough, Joseph Wright designed a new Primitive Methodist church in St Sepulchre Street which was built on the site of a previous church and seated about 1000 people.
References - (14), (44), (84), (85j), (92a) (92c).

WYATT, Henry   **London architect**
1811 (Windsor) - 1899

Scarborough work - Gothic Saloon at Spa (1839, extended 1845), St Nicholas House, St Nicholas St - now Town Hall (1852), Royal Hotel Harcourt Place extension (1862), Woodall, Hebden & Co.s Bank, St Nicholas Street/Newborough, now Barclays PLC (1864).

Henry Wyatt was a son of the sculptor Matthew Cotes Wyatt (1777-1862) and grandson of the architect James Wyatt (1746 -1813) who specialised in "gothic" design and who was appointed Surveyor General in 1796.
Henry Wyatt established an architectural practice in London, although his work was mainly in Yorkshire.
Wyatt's earliest work in Scarborough was to design a saloon at the Spa and, perhaps inspired by his grandfather, he chose a gothic style with castellations. Wyatt's "Gothic Saloon" was opened in 1839 and included a concert hall to seat 500 people. However, the building was soon found to be too small, the original size having been reduced to contain costs, and in 1845 Wyatt was asked to design an enlargement. The contractor for all of this work was John Barry (1803-66 q.v.).
In 1852 Henry Wyatt exhibited a design for "St Nicholas House", Scarborough at the Royal Academy. This was the house he designed for John Woodall (1801-79) which today forms part of Scarborough Town Hall. For Messrs Woodall, Hebden & Co. Wyatt designed new banking premises in an Italian style with a rusticated ground floor at the corner of St Nicholas Street and Newborough (1864).
References - (14), (26), (40), (44), (46), (54), (85j), (94), (101), (106), (118).

WYLD, Robert Stodart   **Scottish harbour engineer**
1855 (Queensferry) - 1891

Scarborough work - Scarborough Harbour extension (1878-81).

Robert Wyld trained as a civil engineer and became an Associate Member of the Institution of Civil Engineers in 1880, a full Member in 1888 and a Fellow of the Geological Society in 1890.

The Harbour Committee of Scarborough Corporation resolved as early as 1867 to improve the west pier, but it was not until 1878 that the plans of the consulting engineer John Howkins (q.v.) were accepted. Robert Wyld was appointed as resident engineer for the project and another Scot, Mr Morrison, of Leith became contractor. The work, which involved deepening both harbours, widening and extending the west pier under-building old quay walls etc. began in 1879 and was completed in 1881 when Wyld returned to Scotland.

References – (61), (64), (99).

Bar St. Congregational Church (1850-1962) by W.Raffles Brown
(see pg 16)

Amicable Society's Schools, Castle Road (1865) by W.B.Stewart (see pg 75)

REFERENCES

1. **Allott, Stephen,** John Wilhelm Rowntree, 1868-1905, Session Book Trust, York 1994.

2. **Anon.** The Crown Hotel Scarborough - 150 Years of Hospitality Scarborough 1995.

3. **The Architect,** "The New Spa Buildings at Scarborough", 7th August 1880.

4. **Baines, Edward,** Directory and Gazetteer of County of York, vol. II The East and North Ridings, 1823, David & Charles Reprints 1969.

5. **Baker, Joseph Brogden,** The History of Scarborough London, 1882.

6. **Bayes, Joan,** One More Step, Westborough Church Council, Scarborough, 1999.

7. **Bayliss, Anne & Paul,** Scarborough Artists of the Nineteenth Century, Scarborough 1997.

8. **Bayliss, Anne & Paul,** Photographers in Mid Nineteenth Century Scarborough, Scarborough 1998.

9. **Blakey, J.W. (ed.)** Some Scarborough Faces, Past and Present, Scarborough Gazette Printing & Publishing Co. 1901.

10. **Bournemouth, St Paul's Church of England, 1881-1981,** (Bournemouth Reference Library).

11. **Bournemouth, St Andrew's Church Jubilee Memoir 1892-1942,** (Bournemouth Reference Library).

12. **Bournemouth Town Guide 1939.**

13. **A Brief History of Burniston,** Local History Group, 1995.

14. **British Census Records** 1851-1891.

15. **British Patent 1852** No. 917.

16. **British Patent 1875** No. 3926.

16a. **British Patent 1894**   No. 16,396.

17. **Browne, H.B.** The Chapman Story, 1327-1954, Horne & Son Ltd, Whitby 1954.

18. **The Builder**, 1843-1942.

19. **ed. Burton, Peter** Six Inches of Bathwater, 100 years of Scarborough College, Memories and Photographs 1898-1998.

20. **Carter, Oliver,** British Railway Hotels 1838-1983, Silver Link Publishing, Lancashire.

21. **Carter, Robert,** A Visitor's Guide to Yorkshire Churches, Watmoughs Ltd, 1976.

22. **The Centenary of Scarborough Public Market Company 1853-1953,** (Scarborough Library).

23. **Childs, John T.**, A Brief History of Seamer & Irton, Scarborough, 1979.

24. **Christian, Ewan,** Report upon the present condition of the Ancient Church of St Mary, Scarborough upon the means proposed for its   permanent stability and for its restoration, Scarborough 1847.

25. **Clarke, B.F.L.** Church Builders of the Nineteenth Century, David & Charles Reprints, 1969.

26. **Colvin, Howard.** A Biographical Dictionary of British Architects 1600-1840, John Murray, London 1978.

27. **Contemporary Biographies,** N & E Riding of Yorks. at Opening of 20th Century.

28. **de Courcy, J.W.** The Liffey in Dublin, Gill & Macmillan.

29. **The Crescent Houses and Rotunda,** Scarborough Borough Council.

30. **Crouch, David**, St Martin-on-the-Hill Scarborough, Scarborough 1992.

31. **Crouch, David,** The History of St Martin's Church of England School Scarborough. Scarborough 1998.

32. **Crouch, David**, The Church of St Martin, Seamer.

33. **Dawson, J.R.** The Church of Saint Laurence, Kirby Misperton.

34. **Dewe, Michael** An Edwardian Public Library Architect, (M.A. thesis - part of), Wolverhampton Library.

35. **Dictionary of National Biography,** (Compact Edition) Oxford University Press 1975.

36. **Directories**
     a. **Scarborough 1823-1939.**
     b. **York 1830-38.**
     c. **Edinburgh & Leith 1853-3.**
     d. **Hull 1905-21.**

37. **Douglas (Isle of Man) Centenary Book** 1896-1996.

38. **Easdown, Martin,** Piers of Disaster, The Sad Story of the Seaside Pleasure Piers of the Yorkshire Coast, Hutton Press Ltd, 1996.

39. **Ecclestone, A.W.** A Yarmouth Miscellany, Ecclestone 1974

40. **ed. Edwards, Mervyn,** Scarborough 966-1966, Scarborough & District Archaeological Society, 1966.

41. **"An End to Picnicking", The Story of County Buildings, Stafford 1895-1995**, Staffordshire County Council 1995.

42. **Fawcett, Bill**, A History of the York - Scarborough Railway, Hutton Press, 1995.

43. **Fearon, Michael**, Filey, from Fishing Village to Edwardian Resort, Hutton Press 1990.

44. **ed. Feldstead A. Directory of British Architects 1834- 1900**, British Architectural Library, RIBA, Mansell London 1993.

45. **Field C.R.** Catalogue of Manuscripts, Scarborough Central Library 1968.

46. **Fieldhouse, Raymond & Barrett, John,** The Streets of Scarborough, Scarborough and District Civic Society, 1977 (revised edition).

47. **Girouard, Mark,** The English Town, Yale University Press 1990.

48. **Goode, C.T.** The York and Scarborough Railway, Burstwick Print, Hull 1998.

49. **Goodricke, Fras.** Scarborough and Scarborough Spa, E.T.W. Dennis, The Bar Library Press, Scarborough 1891.

50. **Gotch, J.A.** The Growth and Work of the Royal Institute of British Architects, A Centenary History, RIBA 1934.

51. **Grant, James,** Old and New Edinburgh, Volume III, Cassel, Petter, Galpin & Co. London, 1882.

52. **ed. Grant, John,** A Thousand Faces, A celebration of the Millenium at Gladstone Road Schools, Scarborough 2000.

53. **Graves, Algernon.** A Dictionary of Artists who have exhibited work in the Principal London Exhibitions, 1760-1893, Kingsmead Reprints, Bath 1973.

54. **Graves, Algernon.** The Royal Academy of Arts. A Complete Dictionary of Contributors and their Work, from its Foundation in 1769 to 1904, Kingsmead Reprints and Hilmarton Manor Press 1989.

55. **The Guide to County Buildings,** Stafford, Staffordshire County Council 1995

56. **Gunnis, Rupert,** Dictionary of British Sculptors 1660-1851, London, 1951.

57. **Harper, Roger H.** Victorian Architectural Competitions (1843-1900), Mansell Publishing 1983. (ex Harrogate Ref. Library).

58. **Haviland, Alfred,** Scarborough as a Health Resort, 1883.

59. **Hinderwell, Thomas,** The History and Antiquities of Scarborough, 1832.

60. **Horspool, Maurice,** The Stones Of St Mary's, Scarborough, 1974.

61. **Institution of Civil Engineers,** Candidates circular submitted prior to election as an associate member, 1861 – 1898.

62. **Institution of Civil Engineers** Candidates circular submitted prior to transfer to member of ICE, 1863 - 1880.

63. **Institution of Civil Engineers** Transactions - Volume 1, 1836

64. **Institution of Civil Engineers** Minutes of Proceedings (including obituaries) - volumes 78, 100, 104, 105, 113, 120, 124, 130, 154, 165 & 183.

65. **Institution of Civil Engineers** Draft Biographical Dictionary of Civil Engineers.

66. **Irish Architectural Archive,** Index of Irish Architects, Dublin.

67. **Isle of Man Victorian Society** Newsletter no. 31, 1991.

68. **Johnston, J. & Greutzner, A.** British Artists, 1880-1940, A.C.C. Woodbridge 1976.

69. **Knowles, George,** Railroad. Observations on the expediency of making a line of Railroad from York to Scarborough 1841 together with a supplement by the same author 1/1/1844, Scarborough 1844.

70. **Lidster, J. Robin,** The Scarborough and Whitby railway, Hendon Publishing, Lancs. 1977.

71. **Lidster, J. Robin,** The Forge Valley Line, Hendon Publishing, Lancs. 1986.

72. **Lidster, J. Robin,** Scarborough Railway Station, Hendon Publishing, Lancs. 1995.

73. **Linstrum, Derek,** West Yorkshire Architects & Architecture, Lund Humphries, London 1978.

74.   **Linstrum, Derek,** Towers and Colonnades - The Architecture of Cuthbert Brodrick, Leeds 1999.

75.   **McNaughton, Patricia,** St Andrew's United Reform Church, Ramshill, Scarborough, Scarborough 2000.

76.   **ed. Magnusson, Magnus,** Chambers Biographical Dictionary, Edinburgh, 1990.

77.   **Marsay, Mark,** Bombardment ! The Day the East Coast Bled, Great Northern Publishing, Scarborough 1999.

78.   **Martin D., Martin S. & Peel A.** Grave Inscriptions, St Mary's Scarborough, (surveyed 1979), Scarborough Library.

79.   **Mason, Philip,** The Hieress and The Architect, Sharow, North Yorkshire, 2000.

80.   **Meadley, C.** Memorials of Old Scarborough, London & Scarborough 1890.

81.   **Minskip, Dominic,** A History of St Peter's Mission, Scarborough (1783-the present), York, 1989.

82.   **Moon, Karen,** George Walton & Co Work for Commercial Organisations. The Rowntree Firms, The Journal of 'The Decorative Arts Soc. 1890-1940', no. 5.

83.   **Mowat, Sue,** The Port of Leith, its History and its People, Forth Ports PLC.

84.   **Neave, David & Susan,** East Riding Chapels & Meeting Houses, East Yorkshire Local History Society, 1990.

85. Newspapers
   a.   **Accrington Observer 5/4/1930**
   b.   **Arbroath Guide & Journal 3/9/1842**
   c.   **Bacup Times, 7/3/1868 & 26/12/1868**
   d.   **Bournemouth Daily Echo July 1939**
   e.   **Bournemouth Graphic**
   f.   **Hull Advertiser 11/8/1826 & 26/10/1838**
   g.   **Morecambe Visitor, 6/7/1898, 26/12/1900 & 15/10/1902**
   h.   **Newcastle Courant 17 & 24/12/1847**

	i.	Newcastle Weekly Chronicle 17 & 24/12/1847
	j.	Scarborough Gazette 1847-1909
	k.	Scarborough Mercury 1855-72 & 1907-1991
	m.	Yorkshire Gazette 1819 -1840

86. **O' Hara,** Men of the City, Hull 1914.

87. **O' Keeffe, Peter & Simmington, Tom.** Irish Stone Bridges,
History and Heritage, Irish Academic Press.

88. **Open to View, The Harrogate District Art Collections,** The
Mercer Gallery, Harrogate 1991.

89. **Pearson, Lynn F.** The People's Palaces, Britain's Seaside
Pleasure Buildings, Barracuda Books Ltd, 1991.

90. **Percy, R.J.** Scarborough, A Pictorial History, Phillimore,
Chichester 1995.

91. **Perrett, Bryan** A Brief History of the Grand Hotel, Scarborough,
Ormskirk 1991.

92. **Pevsner, Nikolaus.** The Buildings of England, Penguin Books
   a. Yorkshire, the North Riding, 1966.
   b. Yorkshire: The West Riding, 1967.
   c. Yorkshire: York and the East Riding, 1972 & 1995.
   d. North Lancashire, 1969.
   e. South Lancashire, 1969.
   f. London, volume 1, 1973.
   g. London volume 2, 1952.
   h. Staffordshire, 1974.
   i. Cumberland & Westmoreland, 1967
   j. Oxfordshire, 1974.
   k. Cheshire, 1971.

93, **Pickup, David.** Scarborough and Its Piers, 1730-1830, A study in
Port Improvement, University of Hull Thesis, 1971.

94. **Register of Deposited Plans,** Scarborough Urban Sanitary
Authority, volume 1 1860 - 1891 & volume 2 1891-1914, Planning
Department Scarborough Borough Council.

95. **Rennison, R.W.** Civil Engineering Heritage: Northern England (2nd edition), Institute of Civil Engineers 1996.

96. **ed. Richardson, Harriet** English Hospitals 1660-1948, Royal Commission on Historical Monuments of England, 1998.

97. **Ricketts Sheila,** Lakeland Country Churches, Ellenbank Press 1994.

98. **Robson Peter,** The Fishing Robsons, Newby Books (2nd edition) 1998.

99. **ed. Rowntree, Arthur.** The History of Scarborough. J. M. Dent 1931.

100. **Royal Academy Exhibitors 1905-1970.** A Dictionary of Artists and their Works in the Summer Exhibitions of the Royal Academy of Arts. Hilmarton Manor Press 1985.

101. **Royal Institute of British Architects**, on-line library catalogue.

102. **Royal Institute of British Architects,** Drawings Catalogue.

103. **Rushton, J. H.** They Kept Faith, The History of Some Yorkshire Congregations, Beck Isle Museum 1967.

104. **Rutter, J.G.** Historic Scarborough, Buildings and Places, Scarborough Libraries and Museums Committee 1972.

105. **Salter, Mike** The Old Churches of Cumbria, Folly Publications, 1998

106. **Scarborough Heritage Trail, I & II,** Scarborough Borough Council 1984 & 1985.

107. **Seymour, Bryan,** York's Other Churches and Chapels, Highgate Publications Ltd 1992.

108. **Smiles, Samuel**, Lives of the Engineers (1862) David & Charles Reprints, 1968.

109. **ed. Smith**, Old Yorkshire, 1899.

110. **Taylor, N.** Victorian Society Tour of Bournemouth, (leaflet), Bournemouth Reference Library.

111. **Theakston's Guide to Scarborough 1862,** S.W.Theakston, Gazette Office, Scarborough 1862.

112. **Theakston's HandBook for Visitors in Scarborough 1870,** S.W.Theakston, Gazette Office, Scarborough 1870.

113. **Thomas, T., Jones, D.F. & Dowson, O.,** All Saints Church, Brompton by Sawdon (Leaflet) 1994.

114. **Towse, A.** The History and the Development of the Port and Harbour of Scarborough, North Riding College Thesis, 1970.

116. **Victoria History of the County of York, East Riding volume II,** Oxford University Press, London 1974.

117. **War Graves on line catalogue,** Commonwealth War Graves Commission.

118. **Whittaker, Meredith,** The Book of Scarborough Spaw, Barracuda Books Ltd Buckingham 1984.

119. **Whitworth, Alan,** Village Tales, The Story of Scalby and its Residents, Alan Sutton, Gloucestershire 1993.

120. **Williams, Muriel & Swiers, Brian,** A Tale of Two Churches, Emmanuel St John's Methodist United Reformed Church 1999.

121. **Wood, Christopher,** Victorian Painters, ACC, Woodbridge 1995.

122. **Ed Chatterton, F.** Who's Who in Architecture, London 1914.

123. **Ed Chatterton, F.** Who's Who in Architecture, London 1923.

124. **Ed Chatterton, F.** Who's Who in Architecture, London 1926.

125. **Francis, Dennis Steadman,** Architects in Practice in New York 1840-1900, Committee for the Preservation of Architectural Records, 1979.

PEOPLE INDEX

97

PLACES INDEX